RECENT TECHNOLOGICAL ADVANCES IN FINANCIAL MARKET INFRASTRUCTURE IN ASEAN+3

CROSS-BORDER SETTLEMENT INFRASTRUCTURE FORUM

JUNE 2022

© 2022 Asian Development Bank
6 ADB Avenue, Mandaluyong City, 1550 Metro Manila, Philippines
Tel +63 2 8632 4444; Fax +63 2 8636 2444
www.adb.org

Some rights reserved. Published in 2022.

ISBN 978-92-9269-573-6 (print); 978-92-9269-574-3 (electronic); 978-92-9269-575-0 (ebook)
Publication Stock No. TCS220248-2
DOI: http://dx.doi.org/10.22617/TCS220248-2

The views expressed in this publication are those of the authors and do not necessarily reflect the views and policies of the Asian Development Bank (ADB) or its Board of Governors or the governments they represent.

ADB does not guarantee the accuracy of the data included in this publication and accepts no responsibility for any consequence of their use. The mention of specific companies or products of manufacturers does not imply that they are endorsed or recommended by ADB in preference to others of a similar nature that are not mentioned.

By making any designation of or reference to a particular territory or geographic area, or by using the term "country" in this document, ADB does not intend to make any judgments as to the legal or other status of any territory or area.

Please contact pubsmarketing@adb.org if you have questions or comments with respect to content, or if you wish to obtain copyright permission for your intended use that does not fall within these terms, or for permission to use the ADB logo.

Corrigenda to ADB publications may be found at http://www.adb.org/publications/corrigenda.

Note:
ADB recognizes "China" as the People's Republic of China; "Hong Kong" as Hong Kong, China; "Korea" as the Republic of Korea; "Siam" as Thailand; and "Vietnam" as Viet Nam.

In this report, international standards for naming conventions—International Organization for Standardization (ISO) 3166 for country codes and ISO 4217 for currency codes—are used to reflect the discussions of the ASEAN+3 Bond Market Forum to promote and support implementation of international standards in financial transactions in the region. ASEAN+3 comprises the Association of Southeast Asian Nations (ASEAN) plus the People's Republic of China, Japan, and the Republic of Korea.

The economies of ASEAN+3 as defined in ISO 3166 include Brunei Darussalam (BN; BRN); Cambodia (KH; KHM); the People's Republic of China (CN; CHN); Hong Kong, China (HK; HKG); Indonesia (ID; IDN); Japan (JP; JPN); the Republic of Korea (KR; KOR); the Lao People's Democratic Republic (LA; LAO); Malaysia (MY; MYS); Myanmar (MM; MMR); the Philippines (PH; PHL); Singapore (SG; SGP); Thailand (TH; THA); and Viet Nam (VN; VNM). The currencies of ASEAN+3 as defined in ISO 4217 include the Brunei dollar (BND), Cambodian riel (KHR), Yuan Renminbi (CNY), Hong Kong dollar (HKD), Indonesian rupiah (IDR), Japanese yen (JPY), Korean won (KRW), Lao kip (LAK), Malaysian ringgit (MYR), Myanmar kyat (MMK), Philippine peso (PHP), Singapore dollar (SGD), Thai baht (THB), and Vietnamese dong (VND).

Cover design by Francis Manio.

CONTENTS

TABLES, FIGURES, AND BOXES

BOXES

ACKNOWLEDGMENTS

First and foremost, members of the Cross-Border Settlement Infrastructure Forum (CSIF) Secretariat—Satoru (Tomo) Yamadera, Kosintr Puongsophol, and Byung-Wook (Andrew) Ahn, as well as Asian Development Bank consultants Leelark Park, Taiji Inui, Ki-Hoon Ro, and Yvonne Osonia—would like to express their sincere appreciation to all CSIF members and observers. Without the dedicated cooperation and assistance of CSIF members, *Recent Technological Advances in Financial Market Infrastructure in ASEAN+3: Cross-Border Settlement Infrastructure Forum* could not have been completed.

Also, the CSIF Secretariat would like to extend their special thanks to the chairs of the CSIF for steering all discussions toward productive outcomes.

No part of this report represents the official view of any institution that participated as a CSIF member or observer. The CSIF Secretariat bears sole responsibility for the contents of this report.

STATEMENT FROM THE CSIF CHAIR

As vice-chair of the Cross-Border Settlement Infrastructure Forum (CSIF) and in my capacity as acting chair of the CSIF, I would like to convey my sincere appreciation to the members and observers of the CSIF for their contributions to this report. Members of the CSIF will benefit from this study, showing how new technologies can contribute to the region's systemically important financial market infrastructure. I am sure that this report will serve as a springboard for the technological advancement of financial market infrastructure in the region. Again, I appreciate the continuous support of members and observers.

Additionally, I wish to express my gratitude to the Asian Development Bank's CSIF Secretariat, including the consultants who assisted in preparing this report.

Seung-Kwon Lee
Vice-Chair of the CSIF
Acting Chair of the CSIF
Director, Clearing and Settlement Department
Korea Securities Depository

ABBREVIATIONS

ABMI	Asian Bond Markets Initiative
ADB	Asian Development Bank
AI	artificial intelligence
ANN	artificial neural network
API	application programming interface
AR	augmented reality
ASEAN	Association of Southeast Asian Nations
ASEAN+3	Association of Southeast Asian Nations plus the People's Republic of China, Japan, and the Republic of Korea
BFT	Byzantine fault tolerant
BI	Bank Indonesia
BIS	Bank for International Settlements
BNM	Bank Negara Malaysia
BOJ	Bank of Japan
BOK	Bank of Korea
BOT	Bank of Thailand
BSP	Bangko Sentral ng Pilipinas
BTr	Bureau of Treasury
CBDC	central bank digital currency
CDP	Central Depository (Pte.) Limited
CNN	convolutional neural network
COVID-19	coronavirus disease
CSD	central securities depository
CSIF	Cross-Border Settlement Infrastructure Forum
DLT	distributed ledger technology
DVP	delivery-versus-payment
FIM	file integrity monitoring
FinTech	financial technology
FIX	Financial Information eXchange
FMI	financial market infrastructure
HDFS	Hadoop Distributed File System
HKMA	Hong Kong Monetary Authority
IAAS	infrastructure as a service
IAM	identity and access management
IDS	intrusion detection system
IoT	Internet of Things
IPS	intrusion prevention system
IT	information technology
KHR	Khmer riel
KSD	Korea Securities Depository

KSEI	PT Kustodian Sentral Efek Indonesia
MAS	Monetary Authority of Singapore
NBC	National Bank of Cambodia
NIST	National Institute of Standards and Technology
NLP	natural language processing
PAM	Privileged Access Management
PBOC	People's Bank of China
PDMO	Public Debt Management Office
PET	Privacy-enhancing technology
POC	proof of concept
POS	proof of stake
POW	proof of work
PVP	payment-versus-payment
REST	representational state transfer
RNN	recurrent neural network
RPA	robotic process automation
RPC	remote procedural call
RTGS	real-time gross settlement
SAAS	software as a service
SBV	State Bank of Vietnam
SET	Stock Exchange of Thailand
SGX	Singapore Exchange
SHCH	Shanghai Clearing House
SIEM	security information and event management
SMEs	small and medium-sized enterprises
SOAP	simple object access protocol
SQL	structured query language
SSL	secure sockets layer
TLS	transport layer security
TSD	Thailand Securities Depository
USD	United States dollar

EXECUTIVE SUMMARY

The primary objective of this report is to ascertain the most recent status of technology adoption by Cross-Border Settlement Infrastructure Forum (CSIF) member organizations—including central securities depositories (CSDs) and central banks in the Association of Southeast Asian Nations (ASEAN) plus the People's Republic of China (PRC), Japan, and the Republic of Korea (collectively known as ASEAN+3) region—and to share that information with CSIF members, thereby promoting technical advancement in the region's market infrastructure system.

This report is divided into three parts.

Following the introduction, Chapter II identifies and examines six key technologies that are transforming fundamental financial market infrastructure: (i) distributed ledger technology (DLT) and blockchain, (ii) artificial intelligence (AI), (iii) big data analytics, (iv) cloud computing, (v) enhanced cybersecurity technologies, and (vi) (open) application programming interface (API):

▶ A distributed ledger is a shared and synchronized ledger of transactions between parties in a network not administered centrally. DLT and blockchain (the most common type of DLT) have sparked interest across industries due to their potential to fundamentally alter market dynamics. DLT is viewed as having significant potential for use in payment and securities settlement systems, including central bank digital currency.

▶ AI is a term used to describe computer technologies inspired by how humans think and make decisions using their brains and nervous systems. Many financial services are primed for AI since they rely on vast amounts of data. Financial trading, banking, and insurance companies have all used deep learning algorithms to automate processes, manage risk, prevent fraud, and gain new business insights.

▶ Big data analytics is the process of identifying patterns and relationships in huge amounts of raw data to aid in the decision-making process. Big data analytics can assist companies in reducing costs, increasing efficiency, and understanding their customers better. For example, financial analytics enable the finance sector to more effectively target consumers, make informed underwriting decisions, and handle claims while minimizing risk and fraud.

▶ Cloud computing is a method of delivering shared and scalable information technology (IT) services through networks using underutilized IT resources. The exponential growth of data necessitates efficient online storage that is accessible regardless of location or time. Cloud computing also enables businesses to respond quickly and flexibly to business requirements and even promotes new business model development. Cloud computing market trends include advanced cloud security, multi-cloud and hybrid cloud, and edge computing.

▶ Cybersecurity is the discipline of defending critical systems and sensitive data against digital intrusions. Cybersecurity solutions are designed to resist attacks, regardless of their origin. Cybersecurity is becoming increasingly vital as our reliance on computers, the internet, wireless network protocols, and smart devices grows. Corporations prioritize cybersecurity technology advancement in a world where attack technologies often outpace defense technologies.

▶ API is a set of instructions that define how one application communicates with another. Unlike a user interface linking a computer to a human, an API connects computers or software programs. APIs are a tremendous resource for rapid development; rather than reinventing the wheel, developers can use APIs to access preexisting features. APIs increasingly enable financial services such as open banking, open finance, and embedded finance.

Chapter III details the extent to which CSIF member institutions are incorporating these six new technologies into their systems. The report's new technology inventory is based on a survey of CSIF members and a series of follow-up interviews. This chapter contains the comprehensive results of the stocktaking, including information on each CSIF member's market systems application of new technology. The findings of the stocktaking can be summarized as follows:

▶ Out of a total of 25 CSIF member institutions, eight CSDs and 12 central banks responded to the survey. Of the 20 respondents, 16 institutions (80%) stated that they have explored, or are currently exploring, at least one of the six new technologies: five member institutions have explored a single new technology, three have explored two, six have explored three, and two have explored four.

▶ Six out of 20 institutions indicated that they have previously engaged in—or are currently involved in—DLT: 3 institutions with AI, 5 institutions with big data analytics, 2 institutions with cloud computing, 8 institutions with new cybersecurity technologies, and 10 institutions with (open) APIs. The top three new technologies that the members are trying to actively apply are DLT, cybersecurity technology, and (open) APIs. Central banks and CSDs in the ASEAN+3 region tend to be less interested in AI and cloud computing technology.

▶ The study showed 38 application cases for the six new technologies within the CSIF member community: 22 cases from central banks and 16 from CSDs. (Open) API application cases accounted for 26% of all cases (10 out of 38), followed by DLT and cybersecurity, each of which accounted for 21% (8 out of 38). While all eight cybersecurity application cases were production-level applications, the other technologies had multiple levels of application: (i) the eight DLT application cases included two proofs of concept (POCs), one prototype, two pilots, and three productions; (ii) the three AI application cases comprised two POCs and one production; (iii) the six big data analytics application cases included one POC, one pilot, and four productions; (iv) the three cloud computing application cases included one POC, one prototype, and one production; (v) the eight cybersecurity application cases were all production cases; and (vi) 10 (open) API application cases comprised two POCs, one prototype, and seven productions. Notably, production cases accounted for 24 of the 38 total cases (63%), given that most cases involving cybersecurity and (open) APIs are at the production level. Also,

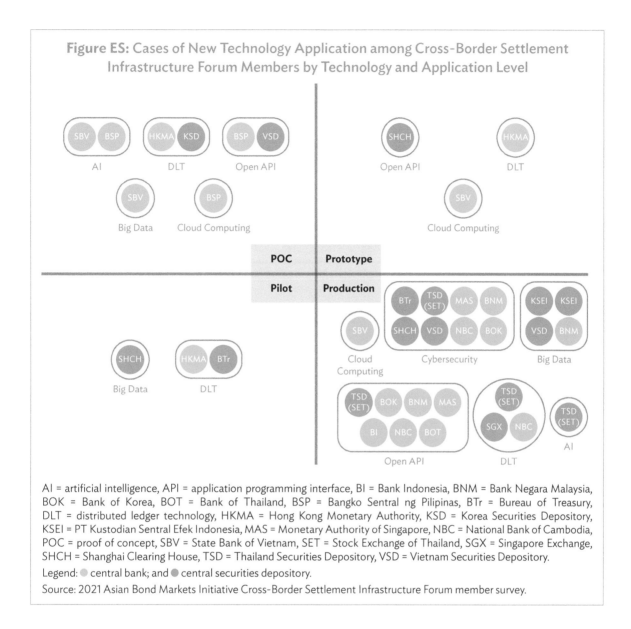

Figure ES: Cases of New Technology Application among Cross-Border Settlement Infrastructure Forum Members by Technology and Application Level

AI = artificial intelligence, API = application programming interface, BI = Bank Indonesia, BNM = Bank Negara Malaysia, BOK = Bank of Korea, BOT = Bank of Thailand, BSP = Bangko Sentral ng Pilipinas, BTr = Bureau of Treasury, DLT = distributed ledger technology, HKMA = Hong Kong Monetary Authority, KSD = Korea Securities Depository, KSEI = PT Kustodian Sentral Efek Indonesia, MAS = Monetary Authority of Singapore, NBC = National Bank of Cambodia, POC = proof of concept, SBV = State Bank of Vietnam, SET = Stock Exchange of Thailand, SGX = Singapore Exchange, SHCH = Shanghai Clearing House, TSD = Thailand Securities Depository, VSD = Vietnam Securities Depository.

Legend: ● central bank; and ● central securities depository.

Source: 2021 Asian Bond Markets Initiative Cross-Border Settlement Infrastructure Forum member survey.

CSIF members are exploring DLT at all application levels, and there are three production-level DLT-based systems in the region. Figure ES shows the application cases of survey-responding CSIF members by application level and technology.

Finally, Chapter IV assesses the six technologies' applicability to central securities depository (CSD)–real-time gross settlement (RTGS) linkages, a regional settlement intermediary model that connects CSDs and central banks in the region directly. Our study concludes that all six new technologies that can be applied to the central bank and CSD systems can also be used in this linkage model, albeit at different times. In the short term, DLT, open APIs, cloud computing, and advanced cybersecurity technologies may be applicable; whereas the remaining two technologies, AI and big data analytics, can be applied as needed in the longer term.

CHAPTER

1 Introduction

The Asian Bond Markets Initiative (ABMI) was launched in 2003 by the finance ministers of the Association of Southeast Asian Nations (ASEAN) plus the People's Republic of China (PRC), Japan, and the Republic of Korea (collectively known as ASEAN+3) to boost the development of local currency bond markets. The Asian Development Bank (ADB) has been acting as the ABMI Secretariat since its inception.

The Cross-Border Settlement Infrastructure Forum (CSIF), which has central banks and central securities depositories (CSDs) as members and ASEAN+3 government officials as observers, is a subforum under ABMI that promotes more active intraregional portfolio investments by creating an efficient regional settlement intermediary (RSI).

Cross-border transactions in bonds and other securities are currently processed through custodians and a correspondent banking network (depending on currency), generating an inevitable time lag between the time of trade and the delivery of securities and money, thus increasing credit risk and settlement risk. To address this problem, the CSIF member organizations agreed to establish a central securities depository (CSD)–real-time gross settlement (RTGS) linkage, which directly links the settlement systems of central banks and CSDs. The linkages among national CSDs and central banks' RTGS systems in different regional markets are expected to facilitate intraregional portfolio investments and the use of local currency bonds as collateral, which otherwise have been locked in onshore markets, by enabling cross-border, cross-currency delivery-versus-payment (DVP) of cross-border securities transactions, as well as payment-versus-payment (PVP) of local currencies in the region without a time lag.

Technological innovation—facilitated in part by the rapid development of enabling technologies such as blockchain, artificial intelligence (AI), and the Internet of Things (IoT)—has been playing an essential role in revolutionizing multiple industries around the globe. Such technological innovation indeed has long gone hand in glove with finance, continuously reshaping the finance sector. Not only do these innovative technologies continually alter what financial institutions do, but new technologies also keep emerging to improve the way financial institutions perform their functions.

Traditional financial institutions, including financial market infrastructures (FMIs), are currently scrambling to streamline or reorganize their business processes in collaboration with financial technology (FinTech) start-ups and global technology firms worldwide. Business processes can be improved in two different ways: by optimizing the efficiency and effectiveness of current business processes or by undertaking complete business process overhauls. Enhancing processing speed and transparency and tracking transactions in real-time without disrupting the existing operational flow fall into the former scenario. On the other hand, decentralization using blockchain technology is an example of a significant business process transformation, as it replaces certain functions in the whole process. Recent technology advancements strengthen the case for the latter approach. FMIs in the ASEAN+3 region have been global frontrunners in such technological innovation.

This report takes a closer look at enabling technologies that are driving recent technological advancements in the finance sector (Chapter II). It then takes stock of the application cases for innovative technologies in the systems of CSIF members and shares the experiences of ASEAN+3 member markets (Chapter III). This report concludes by reviewing the implications of enabling technologies for the CSD–RTGS linkages (Chapter IV). Developing a regional financial market infrastructure will take time, but these disruptive technologies may influence the future architecture of the linkages as well. Our region must stay vigilant for technology-driven paradigm shifts and their possible impact on FMIs.

CHAPTER II
Key Technologies for Financial Market Infrastructure

A. Methodology for Selection of New Technologies

In the midst of the Fourth Industrial Revolution, technology is evolving faster than ever. However, with so many new applications, tools, and techniques available, predicting which ones will be a long-term success can be challenging. This report will identify key technologies that are driving transformations in the financial industry using information from leading worldwide research organizations such as the World Economic Forum, Gartner, and Forrester.

The World Economic Forum's released a report in 2020 that explores eight emerging technologies that will be transformative for the financial services industry (Table 1). In addition, Gartner's 2021 whitepaper explains nine strategic technology trends in the finance sector (Table 2). Finally, Forrester's 2017 report presents the top 10 technology trends transforming businesses (Table 3).

Table 1: Eight Emerging Technologies in the Financial Industry—
Word Economic Forum (2020)

Technology	Description
AI	• AI is a suite of technologies, powered by adaptive predictive power and exhibiting some degree of autonomous learning that have made dramatic advances in using machines for analysis and action.
	• AI will continue to extend human analysis and reasoning capabilities to interface more naturally with humans, allowing financial firms to transform a wide range of organizational processes.
Cloud Computing	• Cloud computing is the delivery of on-demand, remote computing services (e.g., data storage, computing power) over the internet.
	• Cloud computing has quickly become a dominant computing paradigm for enterprises and is the basis upon which future ecosystems in financial services and beyond are constructed.
Task-specific Hardware	• Task-specific hardware (i.e., hardware acceleration) refers to a set of related hardware devices that accelerate and/or optimize the training and inference of AI models because they are physically fabricated to process AI models such as deep learning or reinforcement learning.
	• The development of specialized hardware to augment AI will continue to grow in importance as the use of AI becomes ubiquitous.

continued on next page

Table 1 *continued*

Technology	Description
Quantum Computing	• Quantum computing relies on the physical phenomena of nature to manipulate information via quantum mechanics. • While still in the early stages of commercial readiness, quantum computing holds the potential to solve a narrow, but critical, range of problems significantly more efficiently than classical computers.
IoT	• IoT refers to a combination of hardware and software that allows devices and other physical objects to record, analyze, and transmit data or otherwise communicate with other devices over the internet.
5G Networking	• The fifth generation of cellular networking represents a step-function improvement over previous generations, with the potential to enable use cases reliant on high-velocity data transmission, promising improved speeds, lower latency, and greater network security.
AR/VR	• AR/VR are distinct but highly interrelated technologies that integrate the virtual world with real world. • AR/VR are believed to enable an important shift in human–computer interaction.
DLT	• DLT comprises a set of related technologies (e.g., public and private blockchains, smart contracts) that governs the flow of value and data across decentralized participants. • Developed out of the desire to remove intermediaries by enhancing trust among institutions, DLT aims to achieve consensus among participants to create a common source of truth.

AI = artificial intelligence, AR/VR = augmented and virtual reality, DLT = distributed ledger technology, IoT = Internet of Things.
Source: World Economic Forum (WEF). 2020. *Forging New Pathways: The Next Evolution of Innovation in Financial Services.* https://www3.weforum.org/docs/WEF_Forging_New_Pathways_2020.pdf.

Table 2: Ten Technology Trends for Business from Forrester (2017)

Trend	Description
IoT shifts computing toward edge	• IoT applications require distributed analytics and IoT will spawn a new infrastructure market: edge computing.
Distributed trust systems challenge centralized authorities	• Blockchain will spread to many markets.
Automated security intelligence and breach response unshackle S&R	• Reduces risk and improves security through infrastructure automation
Employee experience redefines applications	• Customer experience insights will unshackle employee potential. • Mobile, social collaboration, AI, machine learning, and other technologies will transform the employee experience to consumer-grade standards.
Software learns to learn	• Machine learning services and deep learning platforms will mature to accelerate self-training models.
Digital employees enter the white-color workforce	• AI and RPA will work together to accelerate complexity and automation tasks.

continued on next page

Table 2 *continued*

Trend	Description
Insight-driven firms outpace competitors	• Amid the data gold rush, a new kind of firm—the insight-driven business—that approaches data analytics differently is slowly emerging. • Instead of focusing on data, these firms emphasize implementing insights in software and continuously learning.
Customer experience becomes immersive	• Customer-obsessed firms are integrating systems of insight and systems of engagement that interconnect people, places, and objects with data to improve the customer experience and forge two-way, value-driven relationships. • Technologies will be used that fuse digital and physical experiences via mobile devices, such as image recognition, gestures, voice, and augmented reality.
Contextual privacy boosts brand value	• Consumers are concerned about data security and privacy, forcing transparency in firms' data collection and use practices. • Customer-obsessed firms will recognize contextual privacy as a competitive differentiator for long-term loyalty.
The public cloud accelerates business innovation	• Firms will make critical investments in systems of insight and AI in the cloud.

AI = artificial intelligence, IoT = Internet of Things, RPA = robotic process automation, S&R =security and risk.

Source: Forrester Research. 2017. *Top 10 Technology Trends To Watch: Forrester Research*. https://www.forbes.com/sites/gilpress/2017/10/23/top-10-technology-trends-to-watch-forrester-research/?sh=4f43f4d42019.

Table 3: Nine Technology Trends for Finance from Gartner (2021)

Trend	Description
Hyper-automation	• Hyper-automation can be enabled by various technologies including robotic process automation, AI and machine learning, event-driven software architecture, intelligent business process management suites, integration platform as a service, and low-code tools.
Intelligent composable business (ICB)	• An ICB is one that drives superior business outcomes by being able to reengineer business decisions and reorchestrate capabilities in a way that is timely, relevant, and contextual to business change. • ICB includes a composable financial management system with a cloud platform, low-code or no-code development, process automation and process mining capabilities that turn event data into insights and actions, and prepackaged workflow and integration with other enterprise applications using modern APIs.
Distributed cloud	• Distributed cloud addresses the need for enterprises to have cloud computing resources closer to the physical location where data and business activities happen. • The use cases are normally associated with low-latency scenarios such as high-speed trading, data cost-reduction scenarios such as data gathering and use for machine learning, and data residency scenarios where law dictates that data must remain in a specific physical location.
AI engineering	• AI engineering is a discipline focusing on the governance and life cycle management of various operationalized AI models, including machine learning and agent-based models. • AI engineering can operationalize the combination of multiple AI techniques from across the organization to create value and tame the AI hype.

continued on next page

Table 3   *continued*

Trend	Description
Privacy-enhancing computation	• To protect data while it is being used to enable secure data processing and data analytics, privacy-enhancing computation comprises different types of technologies such as confidential computing, privacy-aware machine learning, secure multiparty computation, and zero-knowledge proof.
Cybersecurity mesh	• The cybersecurity mesh is a distributed architectural approach to scalable, flexible, and reliable cybersecurity control.
	• The cybersecurity mesh uses cloud-delivered services to provide location-independent cybersecurity controls, encompassing your anywhere operations.
Anywhere operations	• Anywhere operations is a business operating model designed to reach customers anywhere, enable employees anywhere, and use digital technologies to deliver services anywhere.
Internet of Behaviors	• The Internet of Behaviors consists of multiple approaches to capture, analyze, understand, and respond to all kinds of digital representations of behaviors.
	• Combines existing technologies that focus on the individual directly (e.g., facial recognition, location tracking, and big data) and connects the resulting data to other indirectly identifiable information (e.g., cash purchases, automotive telemetry, and device usage data).
Total experience (TX)	• TX is a strategy that creates superior shared experiences by interlinking the multi-experience, including customer experience, employee experience, and user experience disciplines to solve complex business challenges by transforming experiences.
	• Technologies for TX can be grouped into four building blocks: (i) collaboration and productivity; (ii) secure remote access; (iii) cloud and edge infrastructure such as distributed cloud, the IoT, API gateways, AI at the edge, and edge processing; and (iv) quantification of the digital experience.

AI = artificial intelligence, API = application programming interface, IoT = Internet of Things, ML = machine learning.
Source: Gartner. 2021. *Top Strategic Technology Trends for Finance.* https://www.gartner.com/en/finance/trends/finance-technology.

After comparing and analyzing emerging technologies and their trends, as presented by three major research institutions, six technologies were identified as the key enabling technologies with the most potential to transform FMIs: (i) distributed ledger technology (DLT), (ii) AI, (iii) big data analytics, (iv) cloud computing, (v) advanced cybersecurity technologies, and (vi) (open) APIs. IoT and augmented reality and virtual reality were excluded since they are not that closely related to the roles and functions of important FMIs such as central banks and CSDs, despite the fact that they may be beneficial to private financial institutions. Robotic process automatic (RPA) was also omitted since it is different from but closely related to AI (Figure 1). The following section will go deeper into exploring the selected technologies.

Figure 1: Selection of Key Technologies for ASEAN+3 Financial Market Infrastructure

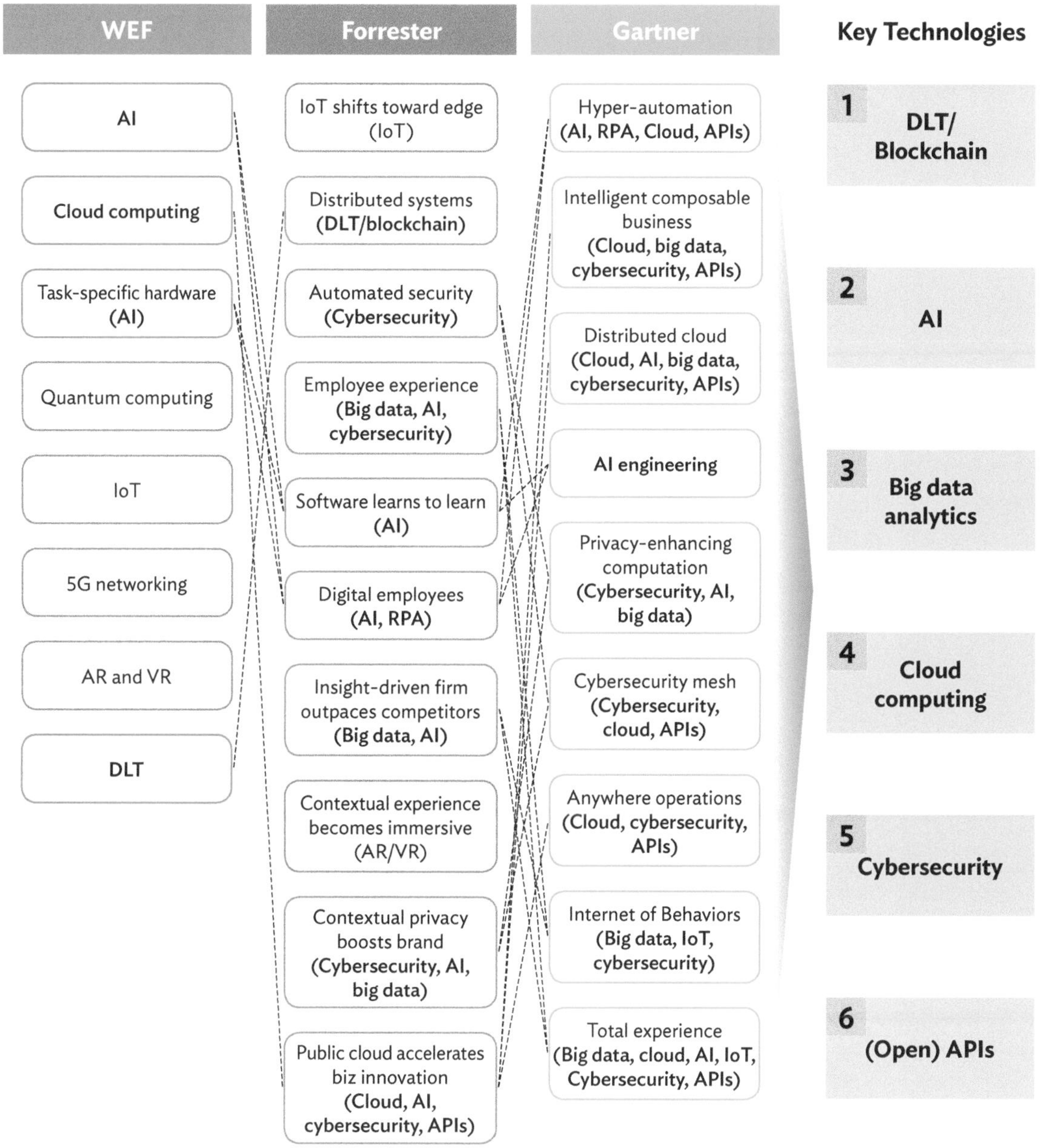

WEF	Forrester	Gartner	Key Technologies
AI	IoT shifts toward edge (IoT)	Hyper-automation (AI, RPA, Cloud, APIs)	**1** **DLT/ Blockchain**
Cloud computing	Distributed systems (DLT/blockchain)	Intelligent composable business (Cloud, big data, cybersecurity, APIs)	
Task-specific hardware (AI)	Automated security (Cybersecurity)	Distributed cloud (Cloud, AI, big data, cybersecurity, APIs)	**2** **AI**
Quantum computing	Employee experience (Big data, AI, cybersecurity)	AI engineering	
IoT	Software learns to learn (AI)	Privacy-enhancing computation (Cybersecurity, AI, big data)	**3** **Big data analytics**
5G networking	Digital employees (AI, RPA)	Cybersecurity mesh (Cybersecurity, cloud, APIs)	**4** **Cloud computing**
AR and VR	Insight-driven firm outpaces competitors (Big data, AI)	Anywhere operations (Cloud, cybersecurity, APIs)	
DLT	Contextual experience becomes immersive (AR/VR)	Internet of Behaviors (Big data, IoT, cybersecurity)	**5** **Cybersecurity**
	Contextual privacy boosts brand (Cybersecurity, AI, big data)	Total experience (Big data, cloud, AI, IoT, Cybersecurity, APIs)	**6** **(Open) APIs**
	Public cloud accelerates biz innovation (Cloud, AI, cybersecurity, APIs)		

AI = artificial intelligence; API = application programming interface; AR = augmented reality; ASEAN+3 = Association of Southeast Asian Nations plus the People's Republic of China, Japan, and the Republic of Korea; DLT = distributed ledger technology; IoT = Internet of Things; RPA = robotic process automation; VR = virtual realty; WEF = World Economic Forum.

Note: Technologies included in parentheses are enabling technologies related to either key technologies or their trends.

Sources: Authors' illustration based on inputs from the Asian Development Bank, Forrester, Gartner, and the World Economic Forum.

B. Key Technologies for Financial Market Infrastructure

1. Distributed Ledger (Blockchain) Technology

Basic Concept

A distributed ledger (as well as blockchain) can be defined as a shared and synchronized ledger of transactions between parties in a network that is not centrally managed by a central authority or third party. Without requiring parties to trust one another, the ledger records and chronologically reports all transactions between anonymous network participants. Without a central authority controlling the ledger, copies of the ledger are distributed among all network members, referred to as nodes, and are continuously and automatically synced.[1] For the last decade, distributed ledger technology (DLT), of which blockchain technology is the most well-known variant, has captured the attention of a wide range of stakeholders worldwide and sparked an explosion of fresh experiments and trials.

DLT essentially uses cryptography and complex algorithms to allow transactions to be shared across a network of computers (participants) and then be authenticated by the participants in the network. The concept of blockchain was originally used in 2008 in a paper about Bitcoin written by the pseudonymous Satoshi Nakamoto. Bitcoin maintains a decentralized database through the use of a consensus-based validation mechanism and cryptographic signatures, and its transactions are carried out peer-to-peer and shared among all users who validate them in bundles known as "blocks." Due to the ledger's organization into distinct but connected blocks, this sort of DLT is frequently referred to as "blockchain technology."[2]

Key Characteristics

While the features of DLT can be enumerated in several ways, the following are some of the more typical aspects of DLT systems:[3]

- **Shared.** The ledger is shared among network participants (nodes). The ledgers of some participants contain the complete version of the ledger, while others' ledgers do not always contain the complete version of the ledger. This ensures both transparency and maximum efficiency among the participants.

- **Distributed.** This means that the database is transparently maintained and stored by all network participants, without the need for a central authority to hold and update the ledger. Each network participant can maintain its own transaction history by processing and validating transactions using a consensus mechanism. Due to DLT's distributed structure, it permits the scaling of network participants.

- **Immutable.** Distributed ledgers are unable to be reversed or changed due to their usage of cryptography, which ensures that the data contained within the ledger is tamper-proof and

---

[1]   A 2017 CPMI report, *Distributed Ledger Technology in Payment, Clearing, and Settlement*, defines DLT as the processes and related technologies that enable participants (nodes) in a network (or arrangement) to securely propose, validate, and record state changes (or updates) to a synchronized ledger that is distributed across the network's participants.

[2]   Bank for International Settlements. 2018. *BIS Quarterly Review*. September. p. 58.

[3]   101 Blockchains. 2021. *What is DLT (Distributed Ledger Technology)?* https://101blockchains.com/what-is-dlt/; Organisation for Economic Co-operation and Development. 2018. *OECD Blockchain Primer*. https://www.oecd.org/finance/OECD-Blockchain-Primer.pdf.

verifiable.[4] If the server or the governing authority is compromised in a centrally managed system, data can be edited or deleted even without the user being aware, and the change may not be undone.

▶ **Append-only.** This is a characteristic of data storage such as a DLT network, in which existing data is immutable. A chronological history of the status of data can be displayed in an append-only ledger. In contrast to typical databases, distributed ledger data cannot be altered.

▶ **Validated by consensus.** In a DLT system, no data value may be added to the ledger without the permission of certain participants in the network. Consensus mechanisms are fault-tolerant rules and procedures for obtaining permission from distributed ledger nodes. There are several consensus mechanisms, each with its own unique set of operating principles, which will be discussed in detail in the next section. Consensus rules are critical in a self-regulating DLT network because they ensure that all nodes agree on the validity and authenticity of all data and maintain the same copy of the ledger. These features strongly incentivize participating nodes to perform honestly, making them a critical factor to consider when constructing a distributed ledger.

Taxonomy of Distributed Ledger Technology Systems

While DLT systems can be fundamentally permissionless or permissioned, their classification in the actual world cannot be dichotomous. They can be classified according to two dimensions: the network's openness and the functions of its players. It can be either a public or private distributed ledger system, depending on its openness, and a permissioned or permissionless distributed ledger system, depending on the level of permission required to contribute data to the ledger (Tables 4 and 5).

Table 4: The Main Types of Blockchains by Permission Model

		Read	Write	Commit	Example
Open	Public Permissionless	Open to anyone	Anyone	Anyone	Bitcoin Ethereum
	Public Permissioned	Open to anyone	Authorized participants	All or subset of authorized participants	Sovrin[a]
Closed	Consortium (permissioned)	Restricted to an authorized set of participants	Authorized participants	All or subset of authorized participants	Multiple banks operating a shared ledger
	Private Permissioned ("enterprise")	Fully private or restricted to a limited set of authorized nodes	Network operator only	Network operator only	Internal bank ledger shared between parent company and subsidiaries

[a] The Sovrin Foundation is a nonprofit organization established to administer the governance framework governing the Sovrin Network, a public service utility enabling self-sovereign identity on the internet. Sovrin has three networks for self-sovereign identity, and each network is based on Hyperledger Indy. https://sovrin.org/.

Source: G. Hileman and M. Rauchs. 2017. *Global Blockchain Benchmarking Study*. Cambridge: Centre for Alternative Finance.

---

[4] The distributed ledger might also be corrupted if network participants collaborate to authorize erroneous ledger entries. However, as the network grows larger, executing this collusion becomes more difficult. Carrying out this attempt in most systems would cost the colluder far more resources than the attack itself would yield. Additionally, some private blockchains restrict access to the ledger to only central authority nodes. Quantum computing (supercomputing) may jeopardize certain existing cryptographic security measures, but it is equally conceivable that blockchain security will grow in tandem with quantum computing capabilities. See also Footnote 3.

Table 5: Comparison between Permissionless and Permissioned Distributed
Ledger Technology Systems

	Distributed Ledger		Centralized Ledger (conventional)
	Permissionless	**Permissioned**	
Centrally managed	No	Yes (Possibly limited)	Yes
Openness and transparency	Open and transparent	Levels of openness and transparency are designable	Levels of openness and transparency are designable in different ways
Identity	Anonymous[a] (Protected by pseudonym)	Identity verification required	Identity verification required
Legal clarity	Low (No legal ownership of the ledger exists[b])	Very high (Legal ownership of the ledger exists)	Very high (Legal ownership of the ledger exists)
Level of trust	Zero trust	High	Very high
No. of readers	High	High	High
No. of writers	High	Low	High
Speed — Throughput	Low	High	Very high
Speed — Latency	Slow	Medium	Fast
Consensus mechanism	Mainly POW, some POS	Any consensus mechanism less difficult or energy intensive than POW	N.A.

N.A. = not applicable, POS = proof of stake, POW = proof of work.

[a] Network participants cannot be completely anonymous with blockchain technology. While participant names are typically hidden and transactions are linked by pseudonymous identifiers (e.g., public keys), on public blockchain platforms their accounts are not, as all transactions and other data are visible to all other participants. These systems enable the creation of user accounts without the need for authentication or authorization. This enables participants to operate in an anonymous manner.

[b] There are legal and regulatory challenges to the lack of ownership in permissionless DLT systems. For example, there is no central owner of the ledger, and all users share identical ledger copies. Permissioned systems, on the other hand, can be more simply integrated into existing legal and regulatory frameworks and institutional arrangements, as the system's owner or administrator is typically a legal body.

Source: Adapted from Jean-March Seigneur. 2019. *DLT Development Platforms Comparison*. https://www.wipo.int/edocs/mdocs/classifications/en/wipo_ip_cws_bc_ge_19/wipo_ip_cws_bc_session_2_seigneur.pdf.

Public DLT systems like Bitcoin and Ethereum are open to anyone allowing them to read (access the ledger and see transactions), write (generate transactions and send them to the network), and commit (update the state of the ledger).[5] In contrast, private DLT systems permit restricted access to the network to only an organization or a selected group of users. The Hyperledger Project and R3's Corda are examples of private DLT systems. Consortium DLT systems are governed by a consortium of businesses or institutions and are distinguished from private DLT systems by their consensus mechanism. In a similar vein, permissionless DLT systems allow everyone to read and upload data to the ledger, whereas permissioned DLT systems restrict access to the ledger to a select group of users. Any DLT system can

---

[5] G. Hileman and M. Rauchs. 2017. *Global Blockchain Benchmarking Study*. Cambridge: Centre for Alternative Finance.

be a combination of these four types of DLT systems.[6] Financial institutions have shown a strong interest in private or permissioned DLT systems over the years since they have the potential to significantly reduce costs and increase efficiency in a variety of operational areas, including domestic clearing and settlements, cross-border transactions, and trade finance.

Figure 2 presents the blockchain models that organizations worldwide had deployed as of 2019. About half of those who answered the survey stated that their organizations were focusing on a private blockchain model.

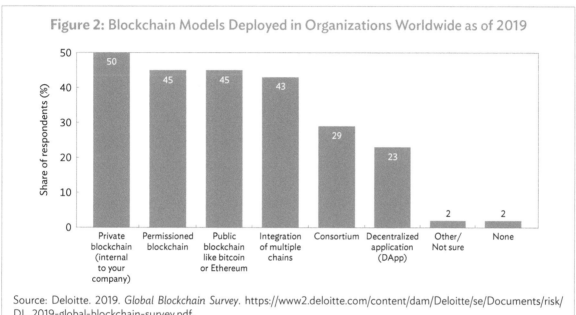

Figure 2: Blockchain Models Deployed in Organizations Worldwide as of 2019

Source: Deloitte. 2019. *Global Blockchain Survey.* https://www2.deloitte.com/content/dam/Deloitte/se/Documents/risk/DI_2019-global-blockchain-survey.pdf.

Consensus Mechanisms

Consensus mechanisms are the fault-tolerant rules and methods by which all nodes agree on validating transactions to be added to the ledgers, synchronizing distributed ledgers across the network's nodes. Deciding which network participant will validate transactions is a critical feature of DLT. The validation process can be carried out using any of a number of possible consensus mechanisms. For example, in permissionless DLT networks, a huge number of nodes compete against one another to validate transactions. There are various consensus mechanisms available, the most prevalent of which are proof of work (POW), proof of stake (POS), and Byzantine fault tolerant (BFT).[7]

---

[6] Hybrid DLT systems combine the privacy benefits of a private (permissioned) DLT system with the security and transparency features of a public (permissionless) DLT system. This is especially advantageous for businesses, as it allows them to decide what data may be made public and what data can be kept private.

[7] There are other consensus mechanisms such as proof of activity, proof of authority, proof of burn, proof of capacity, proof of elapsed time, proof of identity, proof of importance, proof of ownership, proof of publication, and proof of retrievability, all of which are variations on the means for the network to agree on changes to the ledger.

▶ **Proof of work.** In a POW system, nodes must first solve a cryptographic puzzle in order to verify the encrypted transaction, a process that is frequently referred to in the blockchain community as "mining." These puzzles are typically straightforward to validate but need considerable computer capacity to solve. The first node (miner) to solve a puzzle for the next transaction block is permitted to verify the block. The solution to this puzzle serves as "proof" that the node functioned properly. The chance of validating a new transaction block is contingent upon the work's immediate computational power. This prompts massive energy consumption. As compensation for its efforts, the node will earn a specified quantity of crypto assets or transaction fees. Bitcoin employs this technique.

▶ **Proof of stake.** POS is a subset of consensus mechanisms that require nodes to stake a certain amount of their crypto assets to become validators in the network. Validators are not required to expend substantial processing power and are compensated by collecting the transaction fees associated with each block they validate. Delegated POS is a variant of POS in which the responsibilities of stakeholder and validator are split, and the stakeholder delegates their validation roles to a predefined number of network nodes.

▶ **Byzantine fault tolerant.** When some nodes behave abnormally in DLT systems, a Byzantine fault condition occurs—a situation in which nodes in the network fail, and there is insufficient information disseminated across the network about whether the nodes failed. The BFT-based consensus mechanism was created to address this issue by guaranteeing that the DLT network continues to work correctly in the presence of strange nodes in the network. Under the Byzantine fault scenario, it is difficult for the other nodes to proclaim them failed and disconnect them from the system, as they must first agree on which nodes have failed. Therefore, all nodes in the network must engage in the BFT-based consensus process, which entails numerous rounds of voting and communication in order to obtain consensus on a block. As a result, it is more suitable with small-sized permissioned systems, including for a small number of nodes.

Distributed Ledger Technology and Crypto Assets

DLT (blockchain) relies heavily on cryptographic techniques to ensure the decentralized network's security and integrity. As previously mentioned, it was introduced as the foundational technology for the cryptocurrency Bitcoin, which was the first public application of DLT.[8] The original goal of Bitcoin was to create a cryptocurrency ("a purely peer-to-peer version of electronic cash") that would eliminate double-spending (a problem in which the same assets or units of a currency are spent more than once) without involving a trusted third party.[9] The majority of extant blockchains are inextricably linked to a cryptocurrency, which is used to recompense network participants who work on the blockchain in question.

---

[8]   "Cryptocurrency" in this report means a non-fiat digital currency, a form of private digital token, that has three specific characteristics based on a 2015 CPMI report, *Digital Currencies*: (i) it is a zero-intrinsic-value asset such as gold with its value determined only by supply and demand, (ii) it is exchanged through distributed ledgers in the absence of trust between the parties and without the need for intermediaries, and (iii) its scheme does not rely on specific institutional arrangements for peer-to-peer exchanges (no identifiable scheme operator).

[9]   Double-spending in a centralized network can also be prevented via a central trusted third party's validation of the transactions. Satoshi Nakamoto. *Bitcoin: A Peer-to-Peer Electronic Cash System*. https://bitcoin.org/bitcoin.pdf.

Despite their novelty, cryptocurrencies do not appear to be reaching the status of a currency established as a legal tender, but rather are treated and exchanged as investment assets—so-called crypto assets—similar to gold that have no intrinsic value.[10] For the time being, it does not appear likely that they will be widely accepted as an alternative medium of exchange by the majority of nations, given their drastic value fluctuations. They have also raised significant concerns for authorities worldwide since their anonymity has drawn the attention of criminals and terrorists seeking to launder money and finance unlawful activities. Nonetheless, DLT offers a plethora of uses outside of cryptocurrencies, not the least of which is the establishment of fiat digital currencies by central banks.

Smart Contracts

Along with cryptocurrency, smart contracts have been highlighted as a critical component of the DLT system. Smart contracts are self-executing programs stored on a DLT system that automatically execute predefined events or agreements when specific network criteria are satisfied and verified. Nick Szabo first proposed the concept of smart contracts in a 1997 paper, but it received little attention at the time due to a lack of need for their technical implementation.[11] Years later, with the development of blockchain technology, smart contracts were reintroduced as a practice due to their self-enforcing and event-driven characteristics: smart contracts enable network users to be instantaneously sure of the outcome of their executions without relying on a trusted third party.[12] Smart contracts have a broad spectrum of applications, ranging from health care to supply chain management to financial services. A smart contract can theoretically be used to design any action or instruction that a computer can execute.

Since smart contracts are programmed to do a predefined function when a prespecified set of conditions is met, they are particularly well-suited to binary "if, then" scenarios. Nonetheless, AI has the potential for integration with smart contracts. A thorough grasp of the blockchain's rules and policies, as well as an analysis of when and where AI should be used, enables the formulation and execution of sophisticated smart contracts.[13]

Figure 3 illustrates a simplified technology stack, or data ecosystem, for a DLT platform, highlighting the essential technology services required to design and operate a DLT system, as well as the building blocks of smart contracts.

---

[10] Fiat currencies, often known as money in the conventional sense, provide three essential functions, among other things. They serve as (i) a medium of exchange, (ii) an accounting unit, and (iii) a store of value. The value of a fiat currency is defined by the government that issues it and is based on economic policies and the strength of a country's economic system.

[11] Nick Szabo. 1997. Formalizing and Securing Relationships on Public Network. *First Monday*. 2(9). https://doi.org/10.5210/fm.v2i9.548.

[12] Smart contracts can be applied to traditional centralized ledger systems as well, but the design of centralized ledger systems requires such actions to be implemented only after the involved parties have agreed to the underlying transaction as recorded in the central ledger, which can take more time in some cases. H. Natarajan, S. Krause, and H. Gradstein. 2017. Distributed Ledger Technology and Blockchain. *FinTech Note*. No. 1. Washington, DC: World Bank.

[13] In Almasoud et al. 2018. *Toward a Self-Learned Smart Contracts*; and Sander et al. 2020. *Convergence of Blockchain, IoT, and AI*, the authors argue that blockchain, IoT, and AI will converge and enable new business models. They also introduce literature demonstrating the value of merging blockchain technology with other technologies such as IoT and AI. For more details, see https://www.frontiersin.org/articles/10.3389/fbloc.2020.522600/full.

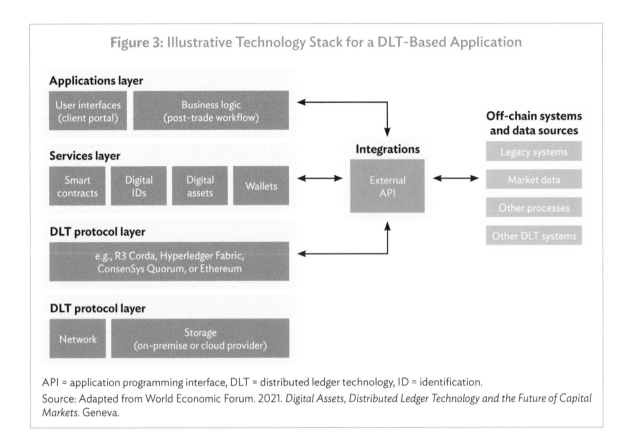

Figure 3: Illustrative Technology Stack for a DLT-Based Application

API = application programming interface, DLT = distributed ledger technology, ID = identification.
Source: Adapted from World Economic Forum. 2021. *Digital Assets, Distributed Ledger Technology and the Future of Capital Markets*. Geneva.

Applications of Distributed Ledger Technology

DLT initially gained popularity to lower transaction costs and increase efficiency in the financial industry, as the early adopters of DLTs were primarily banks and financial institutions. Since then, DLT has sparked the interest of stakeholders across a range of industries, owing to its potential to alter established market dynamics fundamentally. As a result, this technology has seen a broad range of applications in various industries, including finance, trade and commerce, real estate, energy, health care, law, identity management and public records, e-voting, music and artwork, and luxury items such as diamonds. Table 6 summarizes the potential applications of DLT.

When it comes to the development trend of DLT applications, the applications have been developed for various business purposes either by private FinTech start-ups using public blockchains such as Bitcoin and Ethereum, or by industry consortia with licensed blockchain systems such as R3 and Hyperledger Fabric without any related international industry standards in place yet.[14] While most emerging DLT use cases are being developed collaboratively, most jurisdictions currently lack an industry-wide vision for the future, potentially limiting the ability to scale many solutions due in part to significant competing incentives and the risk of value migration across market participants. Also, substantial headwinds—such as unestablished use cases, the need for extensive operational reorganization, challenges associated with connecting legacy systems with new solutions, and concerns about regulatory uncertainty—may continue to impede the adoption of DLT solutions.

---

[14] For traditional information technology (IT), international organizations such as the Institute of Electrical and Electronics Engineer and the International Organization for Standardization provide technology standards and information security frameworks, respectively. L. König et al. 2020. Comparing Blockchain Standards and Recommendations. *Future Internet*. 12, no. 12: 222. https://doi.org/10.3390/fi12120222.

Table 6: Potential Distributed Ledger Technology Applications at Varying Stages of Development

Finance sector	Money and Payments	• Digital currencies • Payment authorization, clearance, and settlement • International remittances and cross-border payments (alternative to correspondent banking) • Foreign exchange • Micropayments
	Financial Services and Infrastructure (beyond payments)	• Digital issuance, trading, and settlement of securities • Repo transaction (bilateral and triparty) • Derivatives life cycle management • Asset and wealth management • Commodities trading • Notarization services (e.g., for mortgages) • Collateral registries including cross-border collateral mobility • Movable asset registries • Syndicated loans • Securitization of blockchain-originated loans • Crowdfunding (as initial coin offerings) • Insurance (in combination with smart contracts) for automating insurance payouts and validation of occurrence of insured event
	Collateral registries and ownership registers	• Land registries, property titles, and other collateral registries
	Internal systems of financial service providers	• Replacing internal ledgers maintained by large, multinational financial service providers that record information across different departments, subsidiaries, or geographies
Nonfinance sectors	Identity	• Digital identity platforms • Storing personal records: birth, marriage, and death certificates
	Trade and Commerce	• Supply chain management (management of inventory and disputes) • Product provenance and authenticity (e.g., artworks, pharmaceuticals, diamonds) • Nonfungible token (e.g., various types of digital files including art, music, in-game items, and videos) • Trade finance • Post-trade processing • Rewards and loyalty programs • Invoice management • Intellectual property registration • Internet of Things
	Agriculture	• Financial services in the agriculture sector like insurance, crop finance, and warehouse receipts • Provenance of cash crops • Safety net programs related to delivery of seeds, fertilizers, and other agricultural inputs

continued on next page

Table 6 *continued*

Governance	• E-Residence • Government record-keeping (e.g., criminal records) • Reducing fraud and error in government payments • Reducing tax fraud • Protection of critical infrastructure against cyberattacks
Healthcare	• Electronic medical records
Humanitarian Aid	• Tracking delivery and distribution of food, vaccinations, and medications • Tracking distribution and expenditure of aid money

Source: Adapted from H. Natarajan, S. Krause, and H. Gradstein. 2017. Distributed Ledger Technology and Blockchain. *FinTech Note.* No. 1. Washington, DC: World Bank.

Figure 4 shows that cross-border payments and settlements were identified as the most prevalent blockchain technology use case, accounting for about 16% of the worldwide blockchain technology market in 2021. Also, IoT lineage and provenance accounted for a more significant market share, accounting for 10.7%. Cross-border payments and settlements have emerged as a critical use case for blockchain technologies due to the vast amounts of money transferred worldwide by consumers and businesses in a globalized economic system. This process has been relatively expensive and time-consuming, as it is subject to the operating hours and transaction costs of the involved institutions. However, the banking industry has emerged as the dominant sector for blockchain technologies on a global scale, enabling individuals and businesses to transfer money abroad at a lower cost. In addition, lot lineage and provenance is another famous use case for blockchain technologies. It enables the efficient and secure verification of the origin and authenticity of product components as they move through the value chain, affecting businesses that specialize in business-to-business software, information technology (IT), and computer services.

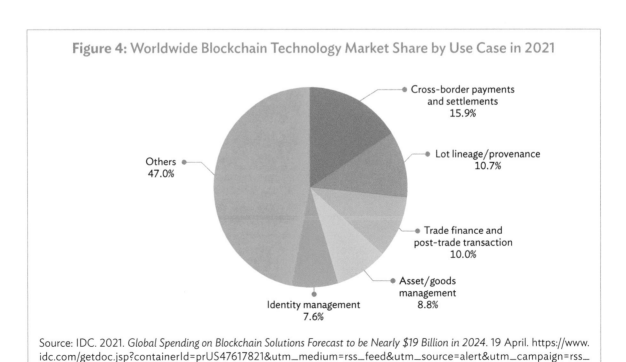

Figure 4: Worldwide Blockchain Technology Market Share by Use Case in 2021

Cross-border payments and settlements 15.9%

Lot lineage/provenance 10.7%

Trade finance and post-trade transaction 10.0%

Asset/goods management 8.8%

Identity management 7.6%

Others 47.0%

Source: IDC. 2021. *Global Spending on Blockchain Solutions Forecast to be Nearly $19 Billion in 2024.* 19 April. https://www.idc.com/getdoc.jsp?containerId=prUS47617821&utm_medium=rss_feed&utm_source=alert&utm_campaign=rss_syndication.

Related to cross-border payments and settlements, financial institutions worldwide have demonstrated a strong interest in DLT since its inception. However, since this report focuses on payment and securities settlement systems among FMIs and the market systems of central banks and CSDs, an in-depth examination of DLT applications to payment and securities settlement systems, including central bank digital currency (CBDC), will be confined to the following two sections.[15]

Distributed Ledger Technology for Payment and Securities Settlement Systems

DLT's distinct technical attributes are believed to have the potential to address fundamental challenges associated with existing FMIs. For example, its shared source of truth across parties minimizes the need for reconciliations and manual data verifications. Business processes automation via smart contracts reduces manual intervention, which increases cost and risk. In addition, DLT enables any real-world assets—such as money, securities (e.g., equities, bonds, and collective investment scheme units), commodities, real-estate properties, or certain types of rights or services—to be issued or represented in digital tokens without involving a central authority. This process by which an issuer produces digital tokens on a DLT or blockchain network, which represent either digital or physical assets, is called asset tokenization. These digital assets may represent only a part of the underlying assets. By enabling investors to invest smaller quantities of money in a particular asset, asset tokenization improves asset liquidity. As a result, economic force backed by recent regulatory progress and technological advancements is forcing FMIs in a number of jurisdictions worldwide to reconsider their business process by adopting DLT. From the perspective of infrastructure development, DLT can be applied to financial market infrastructure (FMI) by revamping existing systems or by constructing end-to-end DLT systems from the ground up.

Currently, securities tokenization is being extensively explored to better understand the value of DLT for securities transactions, especially cross-border transactions, since it has the potential to reduce some of the costs and intricacies entailed in the securities clearing and settlement process. Tokenization, however, does not eliminate the fundamental risks associated with the securities settlement. Nonetheless, it may diminish some of them and alter the way of their management. It has the potential to shorten settlement cycles of securities transactions by eliminating transaction confirmation and reconciliation processes and possibly lowering the number of intermediaries involved in the process, thereby reducing credit risk.[16]

On the other hand, the benefits of tokenization on DLT in terms of operational risk reduction remain unclear.[17] Some market participants may resist shortened settlement cycles since the shorter cycles may imply higher liquidity requirements, thus demanding them to secure the cash or securities required for settlement within shorter time frames. Also, the shorter settlement cycles may result in an increase in legal and operational risks associated with the transition to tokenized securities and accompanying new

---

[15]   According to Bank for International Settlements, FMI includes systemically important payment systems, CSDs, securities settlement systems, central counterparties, and trade repositories. Therefore, the systemically important payment systems and CSDs are the focus of this report. Bank for International Settlements. 2012. *Principles of Financial Market Infrastructures*. Basel.

[16]   Even in a tokenized environment, post-trade processes still need to manage credit risk. There are two types of credit risks involved in securities clearing and settlement: replacement cost risk and principal risk. The former is the risk of a transaction failing to meet its obligation on the settlement date and having to be replaced at the current market price, which is an unfavorable price to a counterparty; and the latter is the risk that one counterparty will lose the full value of a transaction by delivering but not receiving payment, or by paying but not receiving delivery.

[17]   Operational risk is a risk of loss attributed to poor or failed operational processes, people, or systems that can disrupt the normal operating flows of a business.

processes. Apart from that, the legal grounds for tokenization and the subsequent settlement finality must be clearly defined but may vary by jurisdiction.

Securities settlements require securities transfers (the delivery leg) and cash transfers (the payment leg). And most securities are deposited in the accounts of CSDs or central banks in case of government bonds in some jurisdictions and settled either on a single account-based system (e.g., a payment and securities settlement system in a central bank) or across account-based systems (e.g., a securities settlement system in a CSD versus a payment system in a central bank). Tokenization can be used for either the delivery or payment leg of securities settlement or both. By incorporating tokens into securities settlements, three additional DVP arrangements can be created: (i) account-based delivery leg versus token-based payment leg, (ii) token-based delivery leg versus account-based payment leg, and (iii) token-based delivery leg versus token-based payment leg. So, interoperability between account-based and token-based systems will be indispensable throughout any transition from account-based to token-based systems since tokenization of different assets is likely to occur at varying times due to each system's separate management. Moreover, even within a single system, not all assets may be tokenized concurrently.

Distributed Ledger Technology and Central Bank Digital Currencies

Central banks have already issued money in digital form. Still, DLT and blockchain technology, particularly the emergence of cryptocurrencies (crypto assets) such as Bitcoin, has spurred interest in a new type of digital money called CBDC. CBDCs do not have to be deployed via DLT. In theory, more traditional centralized technologies remain viable, but an increasing number of central banks worldwide have been rigorously experimenting with the technology's applicability to their monetary systems. A CBDC can be defined as a new digital form of central bank money, a direct liability of the central bank. It is denominated in an existing unit of account and serves as a medium of exchange and a store of value, but is different from balances in traditional reserve or settlement accounts with the central bank.[18]

There may be several benefits to issuing CBDC: it can enhance operations and cost efficiency of domestic and cross-border payments; provide an alternative to commercial banks' exclusive market dominance; increase transparency through improved know-your-customer capabilities, which can help contain tax evasion, bribery, and other illegal acts; and promote financial inclusion by channeling unbanked or underbanked individuals into official banking facilities. CBDC, on the other hand, may cause financial instability materialized from the risks of bank disintermediation (bank runs) and threatened monetary sovereignty with domestic currency substituted for foreign currency, risks linked with the selected technology itself, and concerns about privacy infringement. CBDC may also expedite financial exclusion by further isolating those who do not participate in CBDC networks.[19]

---

[18]   Committee on Payments and Market Instructure (CPMI). 2018. *Central Bank Digital Currencies* and Bank for International Settlements (BIS). 2020. *Central Bank Digital Currencies: Foundational Principles and Core Features* raised a concept called "synthetic CBDCs," which are issued by private sector payment service providers and matched by funds held at the central bank. This cannot be a CBDC by CPMI's definition but a form of narrow-bank money because it is not a direct liability of the central bank and lacks the profit-neutrality and liquidity of central bank money.

[19]   Footnote 18 and BIS. 2021. *BIS Annual Economic Report—BDCs: An Opportunity for the Monetary System*. Basel.

Globally, a growing number of central banks in other regions are joining the global push toward the development of a CBDC from various economic and institutional considerations, which will influence their policy approaches and technical designs for CBDC projects. According to a series of surveys conducted by the Bank of International Settlements (BIS), at least 68 central banks around the world were researching or piloting CBDCs as of 1 January 2022. Of this total, 43 central banks stated that they were focusing exclusively on retail CBDC only, 23 were working on both retail and wholesale CBDCs, and only 2 indicated that they were currently studying wholesale CBDC. By region, Asia and Oceania had 24 central banks, accounting for approximately 35% of the total. Table 7 summarizes the CBDC projects of central banks across the globe by region.

Table 7: Retail and Wholesale Central Bank Digital Currency Projects by Global Region

Retail/Wholesale	Region	Jurisdiction
Retail Only (43)	Asia and Oceania (10)	Bahrain, Iran, Israel, Kazakhstan, the Republic of Korea, Kuwait, Pakistan, the Philippines, Turkey, and Viet Nam
	Africa (7)	Ghana, Jamaica, Kenya, Madagascar, Morocco, Nigeria, and Tunisia
	Americas (12)	Bahamas, Brazil, Chile, Curacao and Sint Maarten Guilder, Eastern Caribbean, Ecuador, Honduras, Mexico, Trinidad and Tobago, the United States, Uruguay, and Venezuela
	Europe (14)	Czech Republic, Denmark, Estonia, Finland, Georgia, Iceland, Italy, Lithuania, the Netherlands, Norway, the Russian Federation, Spain, Sweden, and Ukraine
Retail and Wholesale (23)	Asia and Oceania (12)	Australia; Bhutan; the People's Republic of China; Hong Kong, China; India; Indonesia; Japan; Malaysia; New Zealand; Singapore, Taipei,China; and Thailand
	Africa (3)	Eswatini, Mauritius, and South Africa
	Americas (3)	Canada, Haiti, and Peru
	Europe (5)	France, Euro area, Hungary, Switzerland, and the United Kingdom
Wholesale Only (2)	Asia and Oceania (2)	Saudi Arabia and the United Arab Emirates

Source: Adapted from R. Auer, G. Cornelli, and J. Frost. 2020. *BIS Working Paper.* No. 880. https://www.bis.org/publ/work880.htm.

2.   Artificial Intelligence

Basic Concept

AI is a term that refers to computational technologies that are inspired by how humans think and make decisions using their brains and nervous systems, but which typically operate in a different way than humans. For over a century, numerous science fiction writers have drawn inspiration from the concept of AI. But it is already a reality due to technological advancements and big data, with machines being deployed at an unprecedented scale across a range of industries. Indeed, AI has begun to surpass humans in several areas, including those requiring cognitive abilities.

Artificial Intelligence Technologies

Machine learning, robotics, artificial neural networks, and natural language processing (NLP) are all components of the contemporary AI ecosystem (Figure 5).[20]

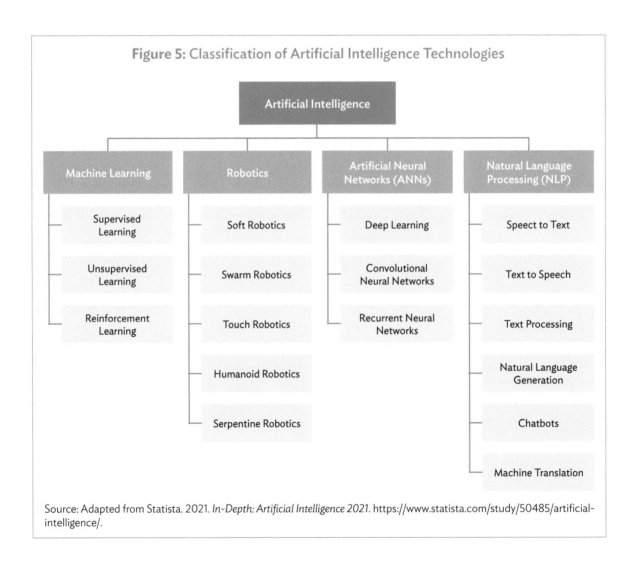

Figure 5: Classification of Artificial Intelligence Technologies

Source: Adapted from Statista. 2021. *In-Depth: Artificial Intelligence 2021.* https://www.statista.com/study/50485/artificial-intelligence/.

---

[20]   This section's taxonomy and conceptualization of AI technologies is based on Statista. 2021. *In-Depth: Artificial Intelligence 2021.* https://www.statista.com/study/50485/artificial-intelligence/.

Machine learning is the process of developing new learning algorithms and refining old ones in order to enable computers to operate without the need for explicit programming. These algorithms enable computers to examine enormous volumes of complex data to identify patterns, make predictions, and make necessary adjustments. There are different types of machine learning—supervised learning, unsupervised learning, and reinforcement learning:

▶ **Supervised learning.** It is a technique that trains the system to respond correctly to specific inputs. Training is conducted by providing inputs and outputs to the learning algorithm, which then learns from the data. The algorithm then makes subsequent decisions using the same set of rules.

▶ **Unsupervised learning.** In this case, the system is not given the correct answer but is supposed to figure it out on its own through trial and error. It accomplishes this by studying the data on its own in order to discover some type of structure or pattern. In other words, the AI system applies the knowledge it has gained from solving one problem to solve a related problem in the future.

▶ **Reinforcement learning.** The algorithm, basically following the principles of behavioral psychology, learns by experimenting with different acts and rewarding or punishing them in virtual reality. It then creates a memory of each experience and applies what it has learned to other encounters in the future. The victory of AlphaGo, a computer program developed by an AI company of Google, against a professional human Go player in 2016 is an example of reinforcement learning in action.[21]

Robotics is the study and practice of developing and training robots to interact predictably with humans and the rest of the world. On the other hand, current approaches emphasize the use of deep learning to teach robots how to wield situations and behave with a capacity for self-awareness. Soft robotics, swarm robotics, touch robotics, humanoid robots, and serpentine robots are all prominent fields of robotics:

▶ **Soft robotics.** It is possible to build soft and flexible robots that can replicate the movements of living organisms, which is what soft robotics is about. These constructions are capable of performing complex movements and are more versatile than standard rigid robots, which are less adaptable.

▶ **Swarm robotics.** A subfield of robotics dedicated to the deployment of a large number of miniature robots that commonly mimic insects or other group-living organisms such as bees or ants.

▶ **Touch robotics.** A type of robotics that allows you to interact with objects. Surgical robots, which are typically employed to do surgery, provide the operator with a sense of touch, sensation, and vision. It is common for them to be created in the style of biologically inspired hands.

---

[21] AlphaGo combines advanced search tree with deep neutral networks, which take a description of the Go board as an input and process it through a series of different network layers containing millions of neuron-like connections. AlphaGo was exposed to numerous amateur games to help it develop an understanding of reasonable human play and then pitted against thousands of different versions of itself, each time learning from its mistakes. AlphaGo evolved over time becoming increasingly stronger and adept at learning and decision-making, a process known as reinforcement learning. For details, see https://deepmind.com/research/case-studies/alphago-the-story-so-far. Another example of AI under reinforcement learning is the Deep Blue, an IBM computer that was developed as early as 1985 and successfully defeated a world chess champion in 1997.

▶ **Humanoid robots.** Robots with a human-like head, torso, arms, and legs. Certain robots may replicate only a part of the human body, while others may replicate the full human body.

▶ **Serpentine robots.** Robots that move in a snake-like way to navigate densely congested areas.

Artificial neural networks (ANNs) are related to the development of algorithms that mimic the activity of the human brain's neocortex area, which is responsible for all thinking. This comparison is not entirely correct, as neurons in the human brain are not organized in the same linear fashion as neurons in ANNs.[22] ANNs are classified into three types—deep learning, convolutional neural networks, and recurrent neural networks:

▶ **Deep learning.** Deep learning algorithms are comprised of multiple layers of neural networks that analyze input at various levels of abstraction. Prior to the introduction of deep learning, ANNs typically had three layers, as opposed to deep learning networks, which typically have more than 10 layers. Deep learning is particularly important since it is the first group of algorithms that does not require operator intervention. Instead, it learns from raw data, in a manner similar to that of the human brain and makes use of a variety of different sorts of sensory inputs. Large neural networks in deep learning techniques continue to improve their performance as they gain access to more and more data, but other machine learning techniques reach a point of plateau sooner. This is the most significant distinction between deep learning and other machine learning techniques.

▶ **Convolutional neural networks (CNNs).** In terms of their overall function, CNNs are extremely similar to conventional neural networks. There is only one distinction between the two: the connections between neuronal layers under CNNs are very similar to those seen in the animal visual cortex, which is the region of the brain responsible for image processing. These architectures have been programmed to interpret each input as a visual representation. In the 2015 ImageNet visual recognition contest, an entry using CNNs has won and even outperformed humans receiving a 90% rating.

▶ **Recurrent neural networks (RNNs).** The architecture of RNNs is different from that of other neural networks. Their neurons are connected to one another, enabling communication through the transmission of feedback signals so that each byte of information traveling from layer to layer can be kept as memory in this network, which can exhibit dynamic behavior. This is the reason that RNNs have been considered to be suitable for the applications of natural language processing.

NLP is a field of AI, computer science, and linguistics related with analyzing and manipulating large amounts of natural language data through computers. It deals with the interpretation and manipulation of human language by computers. Diverse deep-learning techniques are now driving significant breakthroughs in NLP. Deep-learning NLP can now continuously learn from its experiences, and as a

---

[22] A model of AI can be either black-box or white-box. A white-box model is transparent in terms of how it arrives at its results. It is explicable by its design and thus does not require extra capabilities to qualify as an explainable AI (Bayesian structure). On the other hand, a black-box model is one in which AI generates insights from a data collection without the end user knowing how. As a result, in order to make this model explicable, several techniques for extracting explanations from the mode's internal logic or outputs must be used. Algorithms for ANNs frequently take a black-box approach. These neural networks can be so complicated that even if they are shown to be accurate, humans are unable to explain the results. AlphaGo, which was developed using artificial neurons known as "nodes," is a black-box model, whereas Deep Blue, whose decision-making algorithms were transparent and easily understood by data scientists, is an example of a white-box AI model.

result, it is being developed for many applications in wide variety of areas, including finance, health care, and consumer products. NLP-driven applications used in people's daily lives include language translation products, spell check features on word processors, and mobile personal assistant applications, just to name a few. The following are some of the most important applications of NLP:

- ▶ **Speech to text.** In this technology, also known as voice recognition, the spoken language is converted into text that other software applications can process.

- ▶ **Text to speech.** It is the process of converting any text into a comparable piece of speech.

- ▶ **Text processing.** It is a technique of extracting bits of information from the text that can be ingredients for humans to develop meaningful insights.

- ▶ **Natural language generation (NLG).** This technique is distinguished from text processing by the fact that computers use a vast dataset to derive insights without human intervention.

- ▶ **Chatbots.** NLP-powered chatbots can understand a wide range of human conversations. Despite the fact that they are unable to catch the subtleties and nuances of human language, they may be trained to respond to certain types of questions.

- ▶ **Machine translation.** This involves the automatic translation of text from one language to another. This technique has progressed from merely relying on pre-defined rules to incorporating complex statistical models and, most recently, neural networks to simulate human-like reasoning.

Evolution of Artificial Intelligence

Full-fledged AI has the potential to disrupt every industry in the economy, as well as virtually every facet of human life, within the next few decades. The field of AI is now in an exploratory phase, with new technologies and concepts developing continuously. The advent of underlying theoretical concepts such as deep learning and neural networks is having a real-life impact on all industries, businesses, and product and spurring development on all fronts—personal, business, and economic—albeit the coronavirus disease (COVID-19) pandemic has derailed this growth path at least for the short term (Figure 6). A large portion of countries around the world are experiencing a decrease in their working population, which necessitates the use of AI to help maintain and accelerate productivity development. To reap the benefits of lower labor costs, higher throughput, improved quality, and fewer downtimes, companies are currently implementing various AI technologies. From the perspective of economy as a whole, AI-driven process automation will lead to increased productivity as well.

Within these global growth projections that account for the impact of COVID-19, certain countries will have more vibrant activity than other countries. The Atlantic Council's GeoTech Center conducted a study in 2020 and found that technology experts expected COVID-19 to have the greatest impact on AI innovation in India, the PRC, the Rusian Federation, Singapore, and the United States (US). Among this grouping, the PRC was expected to lead the way (Figure 7).

The extent to which automation can be used varies per industry. Diverse factors—such as labor market structure, new technology development costs, the legal and regulatory environment, and economic incentives—will affect the speed and scope of automation. Healthcare, financial services, the automobile industry, and education are the sectors most impacted by AI advancements. As a result, these industries are being compelled to reconsider their business models.

Figure 6: Global Artificial Intelligence Software Revenue by Industry—
COVID-19 Impact on 2019–2025 Compound Annual Growth Rates

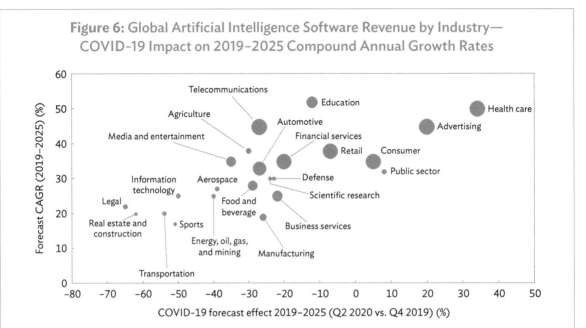

CAGR = compound annual growth rate, COVID-19 = coronavirus disease, Q2 = second quarter, Q4 = second quarter.
Source: Adapted from Statista. 2021. *In-Depth Artificial Intelligence 2021.* https://www.statista.com/study/50485/artificial-intelligence/.

Figure 7: Expert Predictions in 2020 on the Most Impactful Countries
in Artificial Intelligence Innovation over the Next 2–5 Years

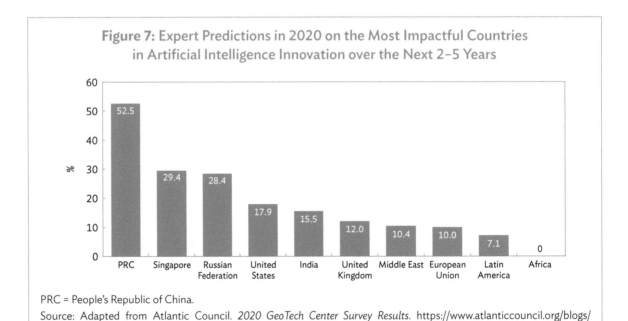

PRC = People's Republic of China.
Source: Adapted from Atlantic Council. *2020 GeoTech Center Survey Results.* https://www.atlanticcouncil.org/blogs/geotech-cues/covid-19s-potential-impact-on-global-technology-and-data-innovation/.

A crucial factor propelling the current AI wave is the dramatic increase in venture capital investments in AI start-ups. The sector is growing due to rapid advancements in computer power and an availability of big data as well. Similarly, open-source platforms such as TensorFlow and Torch capacitate collaborative learning, accelerating the growth of the AI industry.[23]

However, despite these breakthroughs, computers remain limited, particularly in areas such as cognitive reasoning, emotional human-like interaction, and the acquisition of numerous abilities. Algorithms based on data-driven statistical inference impose constraints on what may be accomplished because they can only respond in a predetermined manner to a given situation. When confronted with new and unusual circumstances, they were unable to improvise due to a lack of inherent intelligence, which distinguishes human beings. Additionally, they were incapable of recognizing and expressing human emotion. Furthermore, while AI systems can outperform humans in learning a specific task, such as playing chess or Go, they cannot learn new games or tasks by self-reflecting on previously acquired skills and experiences.

Having said that, a fresh wave of AI advancements is aimed at resolving these obstacles. It has been observed that AI systems are gradually eclipsing humans in a variety of domains needing a high level of cognitive ability. Also, with the advancement of sensors and gadgets that capture facial features, body posture, and speech, among other things, and the progress of AI techniques such as chatbots, emotionally intelligent AI is poised to be one of the most successful AI systems in the future. In the same vein, the development of AI techniques such as graphic processing units,[24] sequential learning,[25] and transfer learning[26]—in addition to deep learning—are taking AI a step further to master multiple skills.

Artificial Intelligence Applications

AI systems are progressively being tailored to meet the specific demands across a variety of industries including automotive, health care, education, finance, entertainment, cybersecurity, online shopping, regulatory compliance, and others.

The financial services sector is an ideal candidate for AI since it basically relies on vast amounts of data. Numerous historical datasets on banking, insurance, mortgages, and financial trading have been linked with deep learning algorithms to automate routine processes, manage risk, prevent fraud, and generate

---

[23] TensorFlow, initially designed for internal research and development by the Google Brain team at Google, is an open-source library software for AI and machine learning. It is applicable to a variety of applications but is particularly well-suited for deep neural network training and inference. In addition, TensorFlow is compatible with a wide variety of programming languages, including Python, Javascript, C++, and Java, allowing it to be utilized in a wide variety of applications. Torch is another open-source machine learning library that supports a broad range of machine learning algorithms and prioritizes the use of graphic processing units. It includes a large number of deep learning algorithms and is written in the scripting language LuaJIT with an underlying C/CUDA implementation. Torch was no longer in active development as of 2018. However, in June 2021, PyTorch, an open-source machine learning framework based on the Torch library, was being actively utilized for applications such as NLP.

[24] Graphic processing units were initially developed for the purpose of producing graphics for display on electronic devices in the 1990s, but they have subsequently been utilized to train large deep neural networks and are widely considered to be a driving force for AI advancement due to their massive parallel design that can perform several jobs simultaneously.

[25] Sequential learning, created by Google's DeepMind in 2017, enables an AI system to retain the neural connections needed to learn a specific task before moving on to another. This technique benchmarked neuroscience studies of how animals continuously acquire new skills by preserving brain connections used to learn previous skills.

[26] To train neural networks with deep learning, a huge amount of data is required. Transfer learning, a novel AI technique, enables deep learning models to train on small amounts of data to address the current challenge by leveraging previous learning.

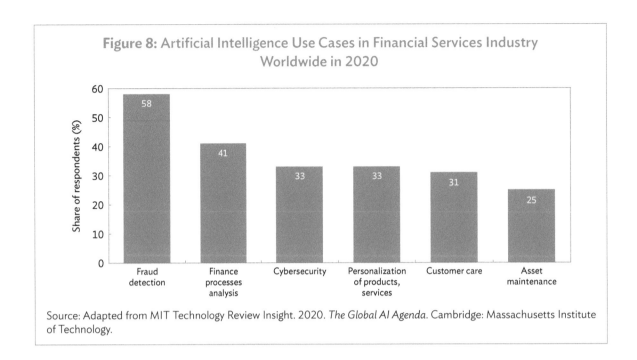

Figure 8: Artificial Intelligence Use Cases in Financial Services Industry Worldwide in 2020

Source: Adapted from MIT Technology Review Insight. 2020. *The Global AI Agenda*. Cambridge: Massachusetts Institute of Technology.

new business insights.[27] Apart from basic AI applications for automation, fraud detection, cybersecurity, and personalized wealth management are also gaining traction as AI applications (Figure 8).[28]

RPA is one of the most widely used applications of AI in the banking sector. It automates most of the analysis work typically performed by unskilled workers. Even though these procedures are highly standardized and formulated, they require many employees to execute low-value-added tasks like reconciliation and aggregation. RPA enables faster processing, increased productivity, personnel redeployment to more skilled tasks, and the elimination of manual errors. However, as previously stated, this kind of process automation built by business process management software is constrained by its inability to react to change. However, an emerging trend is using RPA combined with cognitive technologies including machine learning and NLP to automate perceptual activities that often require human involvement. As they shift to a fully digital operating environment, this combination enables financial firms to automate all spectrum of their operations such as core banking risk management and compliance.

Detecting fraudulent instances has always been a top concern in the financial industry. The spread of connected devices and the rapid digitization of businesses have increased the danger of fraud,

---

[27]   While it makes sense to embrace a black-box paradigm in order to prioritize functionality over transparency, there are still some areas where developers must favor explainable AI as we continue to innovate at a breakneck pace. Many firms inadvertently expose themselves to reputational and financial risk without taking the necessary procedures to ensure confidence in machine learning-based decision-making. They cannot comprehend when things go wrong due to their usage of black-box AI that lacks "explainability" and transparency. Particularly in certain fields of financial services—such as risk management, credit scoring, and portfolio optimization—where transparency and establishing a foundation of trust are critical factors for promoting the rapid adoption of AI solutions in the long run, adopting explainable AIs should be considered.

[28]   While fraud detection was the most dominant AI use case in the financial industry as of 2020, cybersecurity dominantly accounted for 52% in IT and telecommunication industry followed by customer care (48%), fraud detection and quality control (38%), respectively, personalization of products (31%), monitoring and diagnostics (30%).

hacking, data compromise, and other cyber threats. Using techniques such as supervised learning and unsupervised learning that analyze a large amount of data, AI enhances fraud detection capability and helps firms better understand customer behavior. Organizations can better detect and prevent unauthorized or illegal activity when they have a deeper understanding of customer behavior.

While the rapid expansion of the robo-advisor segment demonstrates the growing penetration of AI in the wealth management business, it only represents a small portion of the technology's potential. Robo-advisors, which are digital platforms that offer automated financial advice and investment management services based on algorithms with minimal human oversight, use straightforward, rule-based algorithms to recommend financial portfolios based on factors such as investor age, risk tolerance, and income level. However, future wealth management systems equipped with AI will have the potential to self-learn and, as a result, will give customers more individualized and bespoke recommendations. Due to significant management fees associated with an actively managed portfolio, private wealth management was once only available to selected wealthy people. Using AI, it is now possible to offer wealth management at a very low cost, as the algorithm, frequently referred to as a robo-advisor, monitors consumer purchases and provides real-time advice on spending and saving habits, and determines or suggests portfolio modifications.

The latest trend in cybersecurity solutions is the use of deep learning to enable more extensive and sophisticated malware detection when it comes to cybersecurity. Deep learning algorithms amass a huge amount of data, regardless of its format, and perform tests on it to determine whether it is harmful or not. This data is then sent into an AI engine, which uses it to forecast similar occurrences in the future.

Apart from the ones stated above, AI applications in regulatory compliance are worth mentioning. Financial institutions must adhere to various laws and regulations that are frequently difficult to track. Regulatory reports take an excessive amount of time, and a single regulatory breach caused by an explicable or inadvertent lapse by a financial institution might result in exceptions or even serious violations. AI will consider all regulatory issuances, identify deviations, and facilitate accurate compliance. With AI, it may be feasible to avoid regulatory concerns through the complete automation of operations. Meanwhile, emerging regulatory technology research initiatives aim to leverage machine learning and NLP to make regulations not just machine-readable but also internationally comparable, benefiting regulators and regulated enterprises. Additionally, the development and implementation of machine-readable regulations optimized for use through machine learning may pave the way for the beginning of the transition to digital regulatory publishing.

3.   Big Data Analytics

Basic Concept

The term "big data analytics" refers to the process of identifying trends, patterns, and correlations in massive amounts of raw data in order to aid in making data-informed decisions. These procedures employ well-known statistical analytic techniques or other tools to larger datasets that comprise structured, semi-structured, and unstructured data from a variety of sources and sizes.

Big data is defined as datasets that are too large or too complex for traditional relational databases to efficiently store, manage, and process. Big data has several characteristics, including high volume, high velocity, high variety, high veracity, and high value.[29] There is more to big data than its size. Data can originate in a variety of forms, expand at varying rates, have varying degrees of data quality or accuracy, and carry commercial value. In terms of velocity, big data should be capable of being stored and processed in batch mode as well as in real time. Big data can be categorized as unstructured or structured data. Unstructured data is information that is fragmented and does not fit cleanly into a specified database model. This includes information gleaned from social media, which enables organizations to better understand their customers' demands. Structured data is information that an organization has already managed in relational databases. Data sources are growing more and more complicated, as they are generated not just by humans, but also by machines or processes, such as AI, mobile devices, and the IoT. As technology gets more pervasive, our digital footprints become omnipresent. As a result, diverse types of data must be managed actively in businesses to make more informed decisions.

Since the popularization of the internet in the early 2000s, when software and hardware capabilities enabled corporations to manage the massive amount of unstructured data, the term "big data" has gained popularity. Since then, new technologies have added even more to the huge volumes of data that enterprises can have at their disposal. With the explosion of data, innovative open-source data processing frameworks such as Hadoop and NoSQL databases were developed. This domain is constantly evolving as data engineers seek to combine the massive amounts of complex data generated by various sources, including online networks, sensors, and smart devices. Now, advanced big data analytics techniques coupled with machine learning and cloud computing are being leveraged to extract more complex and unexposed insights.

Types of Big Data Analytics

"Big data analytics" is a broad term that encompasses the collection, processing, cleaning, and analysis of massive datasets to assist enterprises in operationalizing their big data. Businesses can collect structured or unstructured data through various channels. Once data have been gathered, it must be well organized to produce needed outcomes from analytical queries, much more so when the data are colossal and unstructured. After the processing, the data require cleansing to upgrade data quality and produce more robust outcomes; all data must be properly formatted, and any redundant or extraneous data must be removed. Unfiltered data can lead to erroneous acumen. Once big data have been prepared, sophisticated analytics procedures can transform it into valuable insights. Big data analytics is classified into four types:[30]

▶ **Descriptive analytics.** This approach describes past data in an easily-readable fashion. It helps produce business reports, including financial statements. It may also help compile social media metrics.

▶ **Diagnostic analytics.** This type of analytics ascertains the root cause of an issue. Businesses use this methodology because they can obtain an in-depth understanding on a particular issue. Drill-down, data mining, and data recovery are all instances of this approach.

---

[29] BBVA. 2020. *The Five V's of Big Data*. https://www.bbva.com/en/five-vs-big-data/.

[30] R. Pathak. 2021. What is Big Data Analytics? Definition, Advantages, and Types. *Analytics Steps*. https://www.analyticssteps.com/blogs/what-big-data-analytics-definition-advantages-and-types.

▶ **Predictive analytics.** Predictive analytics examines and analyzes historical and current data using data mining and AI techniques in order to make future predictions. It can be utilized on forecasting customer patterns, product demand, market trends, and the like.

▶ **Prescriptive analytics.** This type of analytics is a combination of descriptive and predictive analytics used to suggest a course of action for a specific issue. AI techniques play an indispensable role in this type of analytics.

Drivers

Several factors are driving the current rise of big data analytics, resulting in an exponential increase in data and a commensurate increase in demand to create value from it.

First and foremost, customer behavior and expectations have shifted over time. Customers are increasingly interacting with businesses via the internet and using social media, resulting in a reduction in personal interactions. However, businesses can collect much more information about their customers— such as their browsing history, their location, the timing of interactions—to gain insights into their customers intelligently as well as automatically. In addition, customers are increasingly expecting a high-quality, frictionless, 24/7, customer-centric experience across every possible communication channel. In order to provide more tailored services, a comprehensive understanding of the client is essential, which can only be obtained by exploiting all accessible customer data through big data processing techniques.

Second, technological advancements result in greater volumes of data being collected. As IoT grows in popularity, the amount of customer data will continue to expand exponentially. The recent authentication methods such as biometric and continuous authentication will significantly increase the quantity of data that can be handled in near real-time. Open application programming interface (API) technology that is in the spotlight these days enables financial institutions to gather valuable information on their customers from competitors' data. Also, technological advancements such as distributed processing, machine learning, and cloud computing have made it possible for businesses to process massive amounts of complicated and unstructured data at a competitively low cost and in a shorter length of time.[31]

Third, firms are driven to cut operational expenses through enhancing operational efficiency in order to survive the fierce competition. A large part of these efficiency increases can be attributed to the insights obtained from big data.

Fourth, financial institutions have been under more regulatory pressure. Recent waves of new legislation—including Basel III, anti-money laundering and know-your-customer, and Foreign Account Tax Compliance Act—require financial companies to submit more diverse and detailed information to their regulators, which compels firms to generate an increasing amount of data in a controlled and automated manner.

---

[31] Distributed processing, also known as distributed computing, is a technique that divides a task into smaller tasks that are conducted in parallel over a network of computers, after which the results are compiled.

Lastly, there are growing concerns about cybersecurity as businesses are more and more digitized. This increases the need to strengthen security on the channels for interaction with customers and consumer data via enhanced security tools, such as fraud detection solutions that leverage customer analytics to discover user behavior anomalies.

Figure 9 shows the principal drivers of AI and big data investment, according to C-level executives mainly from the financial services and health-care industries. In 2020, 53.7% of respondents name transformation as a main driver of AI and big data investment.

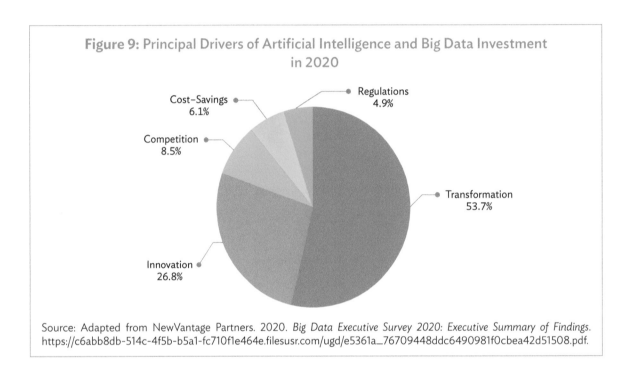

Figure 9: Principal Drivers of Artificial Intelligence and Big Data Investment in 2020

Source: Adapted from NewVantage Partners. 2020. *Big Data Executive Survey 2020: Executive Summary of Findings.* https://c6abb8db-514c-4f5b-b5a1-fc710f1e464e.filesusr.com/ugd/e5361a_76709448ddc6490981f0cbea42d51508.pdf.

Big Data Technologies

A number of new technologies and solutions have been developed to handle the volume, velocity, variety, veracity, and value of the big datasets. Typically, these solutions are built on top of the open-source Hadoop platform. This technology stack enables enormous parallel processing by distributing computational tasks over a number of commodity hardware servers. This enables rapid and flexible processing and minimizes the need for costly hardware. The Apache Hadoop-centric technology stack is composed of several components:

▸ **Hadoop Distributed File System (HDFS).** HDFS is a distributed file system that can handle massive datasets running on commodity hardware. It can scale a single Apache Hadoop cluster from a few nodes to hundreds or even thousands.

▸ **MapReduce.** MapReduce is a critical element of the Hadoop system, serving two functions. The first is mapping ("Map"), which distributes data throughout the cluster's nodes. The second is reducing ("Reduce"), which organizes and compresses the results returned by each node in response to a query.

▶ **Yet another resource negotiator.** This element, a second-generation Hadoop, is a cluster management technology that supports job scheduling and resource management in the cluster.

▶ **Spark.** Spark is another big data framework of Hadoop along with MapReduce but substantially faster than it. Whereas MapReduce is mainly a batch-processing framework, Spark supports both batch processing and online stream (real-time) processing. As Spark does not have a file system, it is usually implemented on top of Hadoop, replacing MapReduce and utilizing HDFS as a file system. However, when combined with a storage layer, Spark can be installed independently.

▶ **Pig.** This is a high-level programming language that simplifies the tasks performed under the Hadoop-MapReduce framework. In MapReduce, programs are converted into a series of Map and Reduce processes. However, this is not a data analysis program which is familiar to data analysts. So, in order to fill this gap, an abstraction called Pig was built on top of the Hadoop-MapReduce framework.

▶ **Hive.** Hive is a data storage system that was developed for the purpose of analyzing structured data. Once data is organized and stored in HDFS, Hive helps in processing and analyzing this data, generating data patterns and trends.

Other than Hadoop, there are more choices of open-source frameworks for large data processing such as Storm, Samza, Flink, and HBase, but they are also frequently implemented in conjunction with Hadoop.[32] Even though the Hadoop technology stack is not a plug-and-play solution desired by firms, it is still one of solutions that many businesses prefer and use.

Besides these open-source generic toolkits available for any business and any industry to define any types of big data analytics, several technology companies have deployed commodity big data solutions, often using the Hadoop framework as the backbone, to implement the specific big data analytic techniques in various industries.

Use Cases of Big Data Analytics

Big data has the potential to have a profound impact on enterprises across multiple industry sectors. In health care, big data analytics could drive faster reaction to emerging diseases and enhancements to direct patient treatment, customer experience, and administrative processing. For communications service provider, big data analytics is being utilized to optimize network monitoring, management, and business performance in order to reduce risk and lower costs. They can also employ analytics to enhance customer targeting and retention. Financial analytics helps the financial industry improve customer targeting, make more informed underwriting decisions, and manage claims more effectively while limiting risk and fraud. For businesses in general, embracing big data analytics to their operations can bring tremendous economic value, ranging from cost minimization and increased efficiency to

---

[32] Storm is a distributed real-time computing system that enables the processing of enormous amounts of high-velocity data in a distributed fashion. It augments Hadoop's batch-processing skills with real-time data processing capabilities. Samza, like Storm, is a stream processing big data framework that is optimized for stream-only workloads. Flink is a similar big data processing framework to Spark in that it allows both batch and online streaming processing. And HBase is a nonrelational column-oriented database management system built on top of HDFS. HBase supports the fault-tolerant storage of sparse datasets, which are frequently encountered when data is collected from a variety of sources. In comparison to relational database systems, which are controlled via Structured Query Language, HBase may be used to manage enormous amounts of unstructured data. Apart from these, various open-source data analytics tools are available such as Grafana, a cross-platform analytics and interactive visualization web application, and Kibana, a proprietary data visualization dashboard application for Elasticsearch.

better insight into customers and an ever-changing world.[33] Figure 10 shows the leading industries based on their share of the global big data and analytics market in 2019. That year, banking was responsible for producing 13.9% of big data and business analytics revenues. The market was forecast to grow to USD189.1 billion in revenue by the end of 2019.[34]

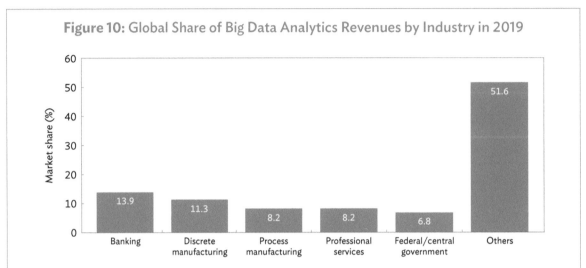

Figure 10: Global Share of Big Data Analytics Revenues by Industry in 2019

Note: Discrete manufacturing is the production of finished and distinct items such as automobiles, furniture, and smartphones, while the products of process manufacturing are undifferentiated such as oil, natural gas and salt.

Source: Adapted from IDC. 2019. *IDC's Worldwide Semiannual Big Data and Analytics Spending Guide.* https://www.idc.com/getdoc.jsp?containerId=US47485920.

In sales and marketing, advanced analytics technology tools that make use of big data provide a more holistic view of customer behaviors. Numerous businesses are collecting and integrating data from internal and external sources to enhance customer service, increase sales, streamline and optimize marketing, and develop products and services infusing their operations with more genuine intelligence. By gathering and analyzing big data, businesses can gain a deeper understanding of their consumers' interests, how their products and services are used, and the reasons why customers cease purchasing or using services. Using big data analytic tools, businesses may more precisely determine what customers truly want and track their behavioral patterns. They can then use those patterns to advertise or provide products and services, resulting in increased customer capturing, customer satisfaction, and brand loyalty.

Big data also allows businesses to create novel, innovative products and services to existing and potential customer by leveraging the insights garnered from data sources. Home and auto insurance combined with IoT, personalized wealth management or health-care advice, and algorithmic trading based on vast volumes of market transaction data are just a few examples.

---

[33] Large internet companies such as Google, Facebook, and Amazon are now processing massive amounts of data on a global scale. Much of the data is fragmented and unstructured pieces of text, videos, audio, and photos that are difficult to search for or process to gain insights. Evolving AI technology now enables NLP of large amounts of unstructured data that was previously impossible. Businesses that employ NLP techniques can access a sizable percentage of their data sitting idle in storage and extract value from it.

[34] Statista. 2020. *Technology Market Outlook 2020.* https://www.statista.com/outlook/technology-outlook.

From a risk management perspective, big data has also proved to be beneficial to businesses, facilitating early visibility into possible risks, assisting in quantifying risk exposure and potential losses, and supporting proactive response to emerging changes. Risk assessment models built on big data have demonstrated their value in a variety of business applications, ranging from consumer and market environment changes to constraints posed by government shutdowns and disasters triggered by natural hazard. Businesses can ingest data from a variety of diverse data sources and synthesize it to gain better knowledge of their situation and understand how to deploy resources to counter new risks. Big data analytics can assist financial institutions in considerably improving their risk management framework by generating enhanced and near-real-time insights from consumer behavioral data. Financial institutions can also gain a better understanding of their incoming and outgoing cash flows, optimize their liquidity management, and improve their credit scoring models for private and corporate customers based on customer insights.

Strengthening cybersecurity and combating fraud are ever-growing challenges for businesses with the advent of the digital age. Organizations such as credit card or insurance companies employ big data analytics to uncover patterns of fraud or abuse, detect system anomalies, and block bad actors. Big data solutions are capable of sifting through massive amounts of transaction and log data stored on servers, databases, and applications in order to detect, neutralize, or prevent potential fraudulent behavior. Additionally, these solutions can integrate internal data with external data to alarm firms about cybersecurity vulnerabilities that have not yet manifested themselves within their own systems. This would be unachievable without massive data management and analytical capabilities.

In terms of business forecasting and internal management support, big data analytics also demonstrates its power. Organizations can now see patterns and trends early on thanks to big data. Identifying shortages early in the manufacturing process, for example, enables firms to respond preemptively, avoiding costly blunders across the supply chain. Early recognition of product demand can aid in improving sales forecasts and determining the appropriate price for a product before it even hits the market. Certainly, big data has aided businesses in making better decisions by providing insight into the possibility of future events. Along with assisting firms in optimizing pricing and forecasting, big data analytics empowers them to streamline operations and increase profitability. Big data facilitates the identification of inefficiencies and areas for process improvement, the elimination of unnecessary expenses, and the reallocation of resources in ways that drastically enhance overall performance.

4.   Cloud Computing

Basic Concept

Cloud computing can be fairly well understood by the definition developed by the Cloud Computing Standards Roadmap Working Group of the National Institute of Standards and Technology (NIST) as follows:

> Cloud computing is a model for enabling ubiquitous, convenient, on-demand network access to a shared pool of configurable computing resources (e.g., networks, servers, storage, applications, and services) that can be rapidly provisioned and released with minimal management effort or service provider interaction. This cloud model is composed of five essential characteristics, three service models, and four deployment models.[35]

---

[35]   P. Mell and T. Grance. 2011. The NIST Definition of Cloud Computing. *NIST Special Paper*. No. 800-145.

The five essential characteristics of cloud computing by the NIST are described below:

- **On-demand self-service.** A cloud user can provision computing elements such as server time and network storage as desired automatically without human interaction with cloud service providers.

- **Broad network access.** Cloud services are available over the network and can be accessed through a variety of client access platforms including laptops, workstations, and mobile smart devices.

- **Resource pooling.** The cloud service provider's computational resources such as storage, memory, and network bandwidth are pooled to serve multiple clients dynamically assigned in response to client demand. Normally, the location of the resources given does not have much importance to the clients.

- **Rapid elasticity.** Services needed can be provisioned and released swiftly, often instantly and automatically, and scaled to customer demand. If more capacity is needed or the increased capacity is no longer needed, it can be added or reduced instantly and automatically.

- **Measured service.** The cloud providers monitor, measure, and report on resource utilization. Customers receive resource monitoring and reporting from the providers and then can pay for what they consumed without the need of monitoring their own usage.

Cloud Service and Deployment Models

As described in the definition of cloud computing by NIST, there are three service models and four deployment models available for cloud computing. The three service delivery models are as follows:

- **Infrastructure as a Service (IAAS).** IAAS provides consumers with hardware infrastructures—such as raw storage space, network resources, and other computational capabilities—on which applications and operating systems can run. IAAS is suitable for tasks that are temporary or prone to sudden change.

- **Platform as a Service (PAAS).** PAAS provides a development environment as a service meaning that it supplies toolkits and various programming languages as well as hardware infrastructure. Customers can use the service provider's prebuilt platforms to test, build, and operate their applications, allowing themselves to work more efficiently in the cloud environment.

- **Software as a Service (SAAS).** It allows users' access to application software and databases via cloud-based clients. Service providers own all physical equipment and are responsible for its construction, operation, and maintenance under this scheme. Users have no control over the underlying infrastructure or platform. This model alleviates the need for an application to be installed and operated on the customer's computer, which simplifies maintenance.

Figure 11 shows tasks and responsibilities in each of the cloud service model compared with on-premises computing stack.

By 2020, global spending on public cloud services reached roughly USD312 billion. SAAS spending comprised the largest segment, accounting for about USD198 billion, or 63% of total global spending (Figure 12). This increase is being fueled by enterprises around the world transitioning from legacy business software to SAAS applications that are more data-driven and more suited to modern cloud

Figure 11: Cloud Computing Service Models

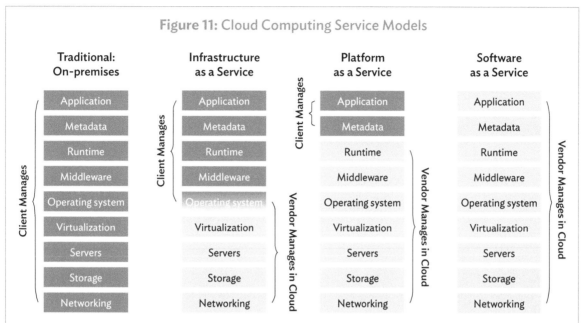

Source: E. Schouten. 2014. *Cloud Computing Defined: Characteristics and Service Levels.* https://www.ibm.com/blogs/cloud-computing/2014/01/31/cloud-computing-defined-characteristics-service-levels/.

Figure 12: Global Public Information Technology Cloud Services Revenue by Service Model, 2016–2020

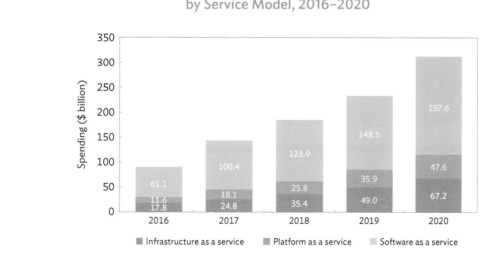

SAAS = software as a service.

Notes: SAAS revenues include both SAAS applications and SAAS Systems Infrastructure Software (SISAAS). In 2020, SISAAS revenues were USD49.2 billion and SAAS applications revenues were USD148.4 billion.

Source: Adapted from IDC. 2021. *Worldwide Semiannual Public Cloud Services Tracker.* https://www.idc.com/tracker/showproductinfo.jsp?containerId=IDC_P29737.

architectures. All of these different service models are offered and managed to varying degrees by third-party suppliers over the internet. By utilizing one or more of these cloud service models and reducing their reliance on running business applications on premises, enterprises can save money on hardware and software. Plus, they may manage applications with greater agility and flexibility while avoiding vendor lock-in.

In terms of deployment aspect, there are four types of cloud services: public, private, community, and hybrid cloud. The public cloud is cloud infrastructure available to the public or a large group of individuals, and owned by external parties. Private cloud infrastructure is dedicated to a single user or an organization. As with the public cloud, the service provider owns the cloud infrastructure. The community cloud shares infrastructure among several entities with common concerns such as mission, security, and compliance. Hybrid cloud is the combination of two or more cloud types (public, private, or community) from one or more providers. The most common hybrid cloud is the mix of public and private cloud. The choice of the deployment model may depend on various considerations of users including purpose of use, technical requirements, financial capacity, or risk tolerance. Figure 13 shows that the share of public cloud services has been growing steadily since 2014 and is expected to reach almost 46% by 2024.

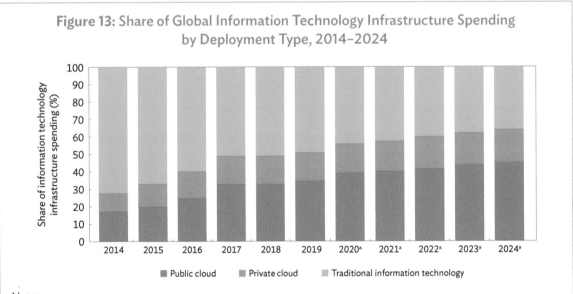

Figure 13: Share of Global Information Technology Infrastructure Spending by Deployment Type, 2014–2024

Notes:
1. Cloud information technology infrastructure products include server, enterprise storage, and Ethernet switches.
2. Overall spending shares exceed 100% due to rounding.
ᵃ Forecast.
Sources: IDC; Statista estimates. 2021 https://www.statista.com/statistics/486586/it-infrastructure-spending-forecast-by-type/.

Benefits and Challenges

Cloud adoption entails both opportunities and challenges for companies. Cloud computing services offer many benefits for enterprises in terms of scalability, cost reduction, flexibility, innovation, maintenance, and security. Cloud services enable customers to rapidly scale up or down capacity as needed, maximizing capacity utilization; require no larger investment in technology such as infrastructure only paying for capacities they occupy; support the ability to test and try out new products and business models, accelerating the adoption of new technologies such as machine learning; and require no maintenance by the customer being managed by third parties. Also, cloud technologies are standardized-location independent, and thus enable mobility improving collaboration and sharing. In terms of security, there exist some benefits as well in that software is updated automatically by the service provider to fix bugs, and data are securely stored remotely on non-transportable hardware.

However, cloud technology also introduces a slew of challenges, including security and compliance concerns, cloud spending management, and cloud migration. Security is a main challenge in using cloud services. Businesses typically store only noncritical data in the cloud, as they lack confidence in public clouds' shared resources. Compliance is another challenge. In today's cloud-based environment, IT does not necessarily have complete control over cloud infrastructure deployment, withdrawal, and management. This has made it more difficult for IT to offer the essential governance, compliance, risk management, and data quality control. Proper IT governance should guarantee that IT assets are installed and used in accordance with agreed-upon policies and procedures while migrating data from on-premises storage to cloud infrastructure. In terms of cloud spending management, cost–savings can only be realized via strategic and proactive planning and management of cloud capacity. Cloud adoption and data transfer can be additional challenges for many enterprises, particularly large enterprises for which the migration process is more complicated than that of smaller businesses.

Market Drivers and Trends

Social and economic developments paired with a robust digital infrastructure indicate that there is an inevitable trend toward more cloud adoption. Every day, we are online with all sorts of connected devices including smart homes and smart speakers at any time and in any location; most of the time even with more than one linked device. This social evolution is true for individuals in both their private and professional lives, and it contributes to the increasing rate of internet penetration.[36] The more time spent on the internet by individuals, the more data are generated. This exponential increase of data necessitates efficient online storage, which can be accessible regardless of location or time. In a professional setting, IT enables businesses to respond rapidly and flexibly to business requirements, and even promotes the development of new business models and processes. IT users are increasingly expecting agile IT that is tailored to their specific business requirements. Cloud computing is a method of delivering shared and flexibly scaled IT services through networks using unallocated IT resources. Several market trends have been recognized in the context of cloud computing, including cloud security, multi- and hybrid cloud, and edge computing.

---

[36] As of 2019, the global internet penetration rate, which is the percentage of total population using the internet on a monthly basis, reached 57.6% and is expected to grow to 72.0% by 2025. Statista. 2020. *Technology Market Outlook 2020*. https://www.statista.com/outlook/technology-outlook.

One of the main topics in the context of companies' cloud adoption and usage is security.[37] While many businesses recognize the benefits of cloud computing, they are still concerned about security. Figure 14 illustrates the growth rate of various IT security segments worldwide in 2021, in which, according to Gartner, cloud security spending is predicted to rise by 41.2% as the fastest-growing segment in the IT security market in 2021, largely due to increased demand for cloud solutions as a result of the COVID-19 outbreak and resulting increase in work-from-home arrangements. Customers are increasingly requesting security solutions for all types of cloud services as they migrate to the cloud. Cloud security is supplied by both market leaders and specialized firms.[38] The market for cloud security is likely to grow substantially in the coming years, coupled with the increase in cloud adoption globally.

Figure 14: Market Projections for Global Information Technology Security Spending Growth in 2021

Source: Adapted from S. Moore. 2021. Gartner Forecasts Worldwide Security and Risk Management Spending to Exceed $150 billion in 2021. News release. *Gartner.* 17 May. https://www.gartner.com/en/newsroom/press-releases/2021-05-17-gartner-forecasts-worldwide-security-and-risk-managem.

Along with cloud security, multi-cloud and hybrid cloud are likely to grow in popularity as a result of COVID-19 as well. Multi-cloud refers to the use of several public clouds or multiple private clouds, while hybrid cloud refers to the combination of different cloud types, both private and public. These approaches become important when a previously used service provider is unable to meet client expectations. To maximize the benefits of different cloud models, such as further cost savings, enhanced business continuity through redundant backup and recovery capabilities, leveraging the strengths of individual cloud services, and reducing reliance on a single service provider, businesses are increasingly implementing multi-cloud or hybrid cloud solutions. Firms can choose the most appropriate model based on their unique requirements, although hybrid cloud models have become

[37]   Cloud security refers to the safeguarding of data, software, and infrastructure in a cloud computing environment, regardless of whether the cloud is private, public, or a hybrid. Security concerns in the context of cloud computing include governance, compliance, the safety of data and systems, including identity and access control, immediate notification of security threats, as well as tracing unexpected events.

[38]   Cloud infrastructure, in general, is equipped with a variety of security measures such as authentication, access control, and encryption. However, this is often an optional service that the big cloud providers do not supply by default. As a result, other specialized service providers offer cloud security solutions.

the most prevalent cloud method. According to a series of surveys conducted from 2017 to 2020, a majority of enterprises are pursuing a hybrid cloud approach. As of late 2020, 82% of corporate respondents reported that their organization had implemented a hybrid cloud (Figure 15). Hybrid cloud has a competitive advantage over multi-cloud as it enables interoperability between cloud types, allowing for flexible cloud selection for any application, dataset, or use case.

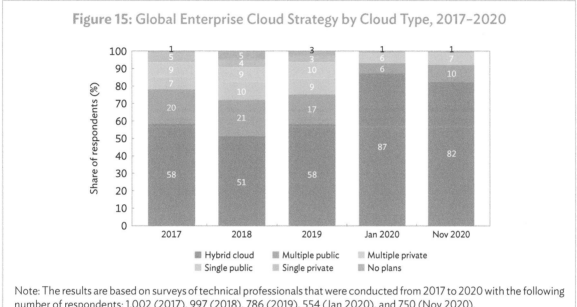

Figure 15: Global Enterprise Cloud Strategy by Cloud Type, 2017–2020

Note: The results are based on surveys of technical professionals that were conducted from 2017 to 2020 with the following number of respondents: 1,002 (2017), 997 (2018), 786 (2019), 554 (Jan 2020), and 750 (Nov 2020).
Sources: Adapted from RightScale. 2020. *State of The Cloud Reports, 2017–2020.*

In addition to these cloud models, edge computing is a new technology trend that responds to the demand for real-time data processing close to the edge device, without requiring data to be routed across a network via cloud-based capacity. While cloud computing centralizes data processing, edge computing distributes data analysis and processing throughout a distributed computing environment. The growing usage of smart devices results in an unprecedented volume of data creation. However, not all of that data is necessarily essential. If end devices are intelligent enough to process nonessential data locally, they can only stream the most critical data to the cloud. Edge computing processes data close to the source, eliminating the need to upload data to the cloud or an on-premises data center. As a result, network and server workloads and processing times can be considerably lowered, and the reduced amount of data transferred over a network can be another tangible benefit from security perspective. Edge computing is well-suited for IoT and offers substantial potential for business innovation along with emerging technologies such as AI. According to a survey of global mobility decision-makers conducted in 2019 (Figure 16), the manufacturing industry had the most interest in adoption edge computing, and 15% of respondents from the financial industry said that their organizations planned to implement the technology in 2020 and a further 28% showed interest in doing so.

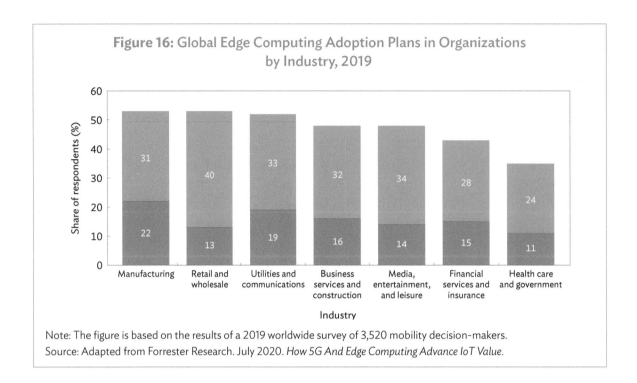

Figure 16: Global Edge Computing Adoption Plans in Organizations by Industry, 2019

Note: The figure is based on the results of a 2019 worldwide survey of 3,520 mobility decision-makers.
Source: Adapted from Forrester Research. July 2020. *How 5G And Edge Computing Advance IoT Value.*

5. Cybersecurity

Basic Concept

Cybersecurity, often referred to as IT security, is the discipline of defending key systems and sensitive data against digital intrusions. These cyberattacks are typically directed at gaining access to, altering, or destroying sensitive data; taking money from users; or interfering with legitimate corporate operating procedures. Cybersecurity measures are intended to counter threats against interconnected systems and applications, regardless of whether the threats originate from within or externally.

The most confounding aspect of cybersecurity is the ever-changing nature of security concerns. IT security is becoming more critical as our reliance on computer systems, the internet, and wireless network standards such as Wi-Fi continues to grow, as well as amid the proliferation of smart devices including mobile devices and various gadgets comprising the IoT. Cybersecurity is also a major concern in today's society, owing to its technological complexity in an environment where attack technologies often exceed defense technologies.

IBM's 2021 report, *Cost of a Data Breach*, revealed that the average cost of a data breach was a staggering USD4.24 million and took an average of 287 days to contain. Further, the ramifications of a data breach can last for years. The expenses of cybercrime include the loss of actual monetary assets, sensitive private information, and intellectual property, as well as business process disruptions, deteriorated business productivity, and damage in terms of brand reputation, among other things. In addition to these tangible costs, cybercrime's extra costs include elevated insurance rates, diminished credit scores, and legal expenses associated with consumer litigation. Complexity and imbalance in a company's overall security framework, resulting from discordant cybersecurity technologies and a lack of internal expertise and experience, can exacerbate these expenses. However, businesses that have a comprehensive and effective cybersecurity strategy guided by best market practices and have automated their security systems with advanced technologies such as AI can combat cybersecurity threats more effectively and minimize the repercussions of breaches that inevitably do occur.

Types of Cybersecurity Threats
While cybersecurity professionals work diligently to patch security breaches, attackers are constantly seeking for new ways to circumvent protection measures and exploit emerging vulnerabilities. Cyber-criminals keep inventing new skills, manipulating work-from-home movements, remote access tools, and spreading cloud services. Among these evolving and evolving risks are the following:

▶ **Malware.** It refers to forms of malicious software such as viruses, worms, Trojans, ransomware, spyware, adware, botnets, and structured query language (SQL) injection that allow for unauthorized access or cause harm to a network or a computing device.[39] Malware attacks are increasingly designed to avoid detection by commonly used intrusion detection tools, such as antivirus software, that scan for malicious file attachments. Global data collected during 2020 indicate that most corporate networks affected by malware were attacked, particularly by botnets and crypto miners.[40] Despite being a relative newcomer in the world of cybersecurity threat, hostile crypto-mining, or "crypto-jacking," is rapidly growing in popularity as one of the most prevalent types of malwares identified worldwide.

▶ **Social engineering.** Social engineering is a broad term that refers to a variety of malevolent operations carried out via human interaction. It employs psychological manipulation to dupe users into making security errors or disclosing sensitive data. Social engineering assaults include phishing, drive-by downloads, and watering hole attacks.[41]

▶ **Advanced persistent threats.** These are a type of cyber threat in which an intruder or group of intruders penetrate a system and remain stealthy for an extended length of time. By leaving the system intact throughout the ambush, the intruder can conduct espionage on corporate activity and steal valuable information without triggering defiance mechanism.

▶ **Distributed denial-of-service attacks.** These attacks are a subclass of denial-of-service attacks in which attackers prohibit a computer system from performing legitimate requests by flooding

39 A computer virus uses a stand-alone vehicle software to implant malicious codes into the program. A worm is a singular piece of software that self-replicates and spreads from computer to computer. The Trojan does not reproduce but masquerades itself as a legitimate program. When a user clicks on the fraudulent execution file, the malware gets implanted into the system and begins wreaking havoc. Ransomware is a malware that encrypts data or systems and threatens to delete or destroy the encrypted—or to make sensitive information public—unless cybercriminals behind the attack are paid a ransom. Spyware snoops and collects data from users' computer systems. Occasionally, spyware will capture user's keystrokes or monitor the data sent and received online. Adware is advertising software made for malware dissemination. Botnet, a compound word of "robot" and "network," are a network of compromised computers, mobile devices, or IoT devices that are used to perpetrate various cyberattacks. A hacker or a group of hackers controls the compromised computers (bots) to orchestrate mass attacks such as data theft, server crash, and malware dissemination. SQL injection is a covert attack of gaining control of and stealing information from a database. Cybercriminals exploit vulnerabilities in data-driven applications to inject malicious code into a database via a malicious SQL statement. This grants them access to the valuable data in the database.

40 Check Point Software Technologies. 2021. *Cyber Security Report 2021.* p. 35. https://www.checkpoint.com/pages/cyber-security-report-2021/.

41 Phishing is a technique used to dupe individuals into disclosing personal or sensitive information. In phishing scams, a perpetrator sends emails or text messages purporting to be from a legitimate business, requesting sensitive information such as credit card or prodding the recipient to download or install software that serves no purpose other than to benefit the perpetrator or is malware. A drive-by download is when malicious code is unintentionally downloaded into a computer or mobile device, exposing users to a range of risks. What distinguishes this form of attack from others is that the download can be initiated automatically by just visiting or exploring a webpage. A watering hole attack is also a security exploit scheme in which an attacker attempts to jeopardize a specified group of end users by infecting webpages identified to be visited by those group members.

websites, networks, or servers with bogus traffic. A distributed-denial-of-service assault often involves a network of connected devices, which are collectively referred to as a botnet.

▶ **Man-in-the-middle attacks.** It is a type of data exfiltration attack in which a cybercriminal intercepts communications between two parties to steal valuable information. For instance, a cybercriminal can hijack data being transmitted between a client device and the network on an insecure wireless network.

▶ **Secure sockets layer (SSL) and transport layer security (TLS) encrypted threats.** SSL is the industry-standard technology for encrypting all sorts of internet traffic, ensuring secure communication between two systems, and keeping cybercriminals from reading the data as it travels through the connection. TLS is an upgraded version of SSL. Cybercriminals often use SSL or TLS to encrypt traffic between their servers and malware implanted in the systems of their targets.

▶ **Zero-day attacks.** Software applications often have vulnerabilities. These are inadvertent defects or weaknesses in computer applications that could conceivably be exploited. If an attacker successfully exploits a vulnerability prior to developers discovering a fix, the attack is referred to as a zero-day attack.

▶ **Insider threats.** If current or former employees, business partners, or anyone that has had access to systems or networks previously abuse their access credentials, they can be deemed insider threats. Security solutions designed for detecting and blocking external threats can be blind to insider threats.

According to a 2021 report by CyberEdge, *Cyberthreat Defense Report*, malware was chosen by IT security professionals as the most concerning cyber threat in 2020, garnering a score of 4.04 on a 5-point scale. Phishing and ransomware were tied for second with scores of 3.99 each (Figure 17).

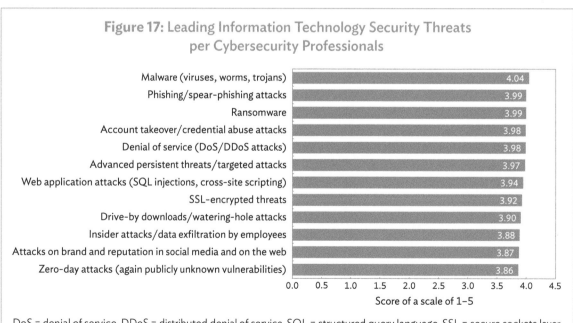

Figure 17: Leading Information Technology Security Threats per Cybersecurity Professionals

Threat	Score
Malware (viruses, worms, trojans)	4.04
Phishing/spear-phishing attacks	3.99
Ransomware	3.99
Account takeover/credential abuse attacks	3.98
Denial of service (DoS/DDoS attacks)	3.98
Advanced persistent threats/targeted attacks	3.97
Web application attacks (SQL injections, cross-site scripting)	3.94
SSL-encrypted threats	3.92
Drive-by downloads/watering-hole attacks	3.90
Insider attacks/data exfiltration by employees	3.88
Attacks on brand and reputation in social media and on the web	3.87
Zero-day attacks (again publicly unknown vulnerabilities)	3.86

Score of a scale of 1–5

DoS = denial of service, DDoS = distributed denial of service, SQL = structured query language, SSL = secure sockets layer.
Source: CyberEdge. 2021. *2022 Cyberthreat Defense Report.* https://www.isc2.org/-/media/ISC2/Research/Cyberthreat-Defense-Report/2021/CyberEdge-2021-CDR-Report-v10--ISC2-Edition.ashx.

Cybersecurity Elements

For efficient cybersecurity, an organization's actions must be integrated and harmonized across all of its IT systems. A solid cybersecurity strategy incorporates many layers of defense measures to fight against various cyberattacks. Cybersecurity can be subdivided into several common elements:

▶ **Network security.** It refers to technologies and processes for protecting a computer network from intruders. Some of the key concepts include network access control and authentication, policy enforcement, threat protection, privacy, secure connectivity, endpoint security, vulnerability assessment and monitoring, encryption, and data loss prevention.[42]

▶ **Application security.** It is the process of building and adding security protocols into applications in order to protect them against security vulnerabilities. It encompasses the security considerations that occur at the time of application design and development.

▶ **Data security.** It is the process of safeguarding the integrity and privacy of digital information throughout its life cycle against illegal access, manipulation, or stealing. Since networks and applications comprise data, it may involve all facets of information security from the physical security of hardware devices to administrative and access controls, as well as the logical security of software applications. It could also include corporate data security policies and rules.

▶ **Cloud security.** It consists of a collection of policies, controls, procedures, and technologies that all operate in concert to safeguard cloud-based infrastructure and data. It encompasses supporting regulatory compliance and protecting customers' privacy as well.

▶ **Operational security.** It includes the processes and decisions governing the management and protection of data assets, the procedures for data storing and sharing, and the network access permissions granted to users (identity management).

▶ **Infrastructure and database security.** It is about protecting physical equipment such as servers, database, and storages.

▶ **Disaster recovery and business continuity planning.** These are rules and procedures for responding swiftly and effectively to unanticipated security incidents with minimal impact on critical business operations. Examples include cyberattacks, disasters triggered by natural hazard, and unexpected power disruptions.

▶ **End-user security awareness education.** It is about crafting a culture of security awareness throughout the organization in order to empower the first line of IT security defense: employees.

---

[42] Endpoint refers to any device that connects to the network, from servers to desktops, fixed function to mobile devices, and any device that is network-enabled, encompassing everything from home automation systems to public safety and personal health devices as well as industrial controls systems to transport systems and devices.

Figure 18 shows the increase in global IT security spending from 2017 to 2021. The majority of spending was on security services, infrastructure protection, and network security equipment.

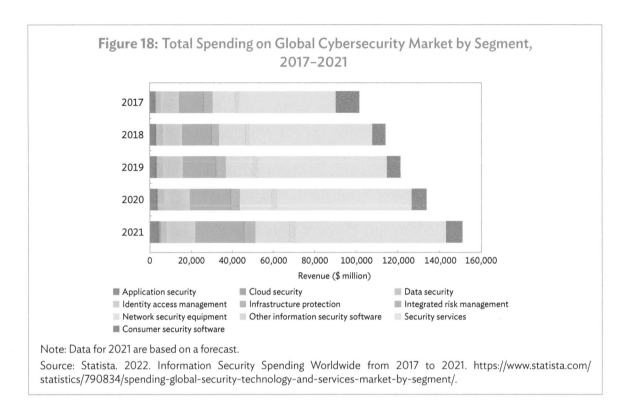

Figure 18: Total Spending on Global Cybersecurity Market by Segment, 2017–2021

Revenue ($ million)

- Application security
- Identity access management
- Network security equipment
- Consumer security software
- Cloud security
- Infrastructure protection
- Other information security software
- Data security
- Integrated risk management
- Security services

Note: Data for 2021 are based on a forecast.

Source: Statista. 2022. Information Security Spending Worldwide from 2017 to 2021. https://www.statista.com/statistics/790834/spending-global-security-technology-and-services-market-by-segment/.

Cybersecurity Practices and Technologies

The following practices or technologies can assist businesses in creating robust layers of cybersecurity systems that mitigate cybersecurity risks and secure important IT systems:[43]

▶ **Identity and access management (IAM).** Organizations can use IAM to create and alter access privileges of users, monitor and report on user activity, and enforce internal compliance policies and external regulatory requirements to safeguard data security and privacy. An IAM solution may consist of a number of processes and tools, including a network access control tool, which enables IT administrators to control network access through functionalities such as policy life cycle management, guest networking access, and security posture checks. Additionally, IAM solutions can provide a broader and deeper view of suspicious activity on end-user devices. This expedites the investigation and response process to isolate and contain the damage of a breach. IAM systems can be implemented as cloud services or on-premises, or as hybrid solutions combining on-premises and cloud capabilities.

▶ **Behavioral monitoring (profiling).** It is a technique for detecting abnormal user behavior on a computer or network. A behavioral monitoring system gathers and analyzes data in order to develop profiles for specific user types based on their role or location. Once profiles are created and activated, substantial deviations from the profiles alert security analysts to the need for additional assessment.

---

[43] The description on each practice or technology delivers only the overall capabilities of a tool set. Therefore, the specifics and capabilities of a system can vary greatly depending on the implementation.

▶ **Mobile Device Management.** This is the process of strengthening corporate network security by controlling and monitoring the corporate mobile devices such as laptops, smartphones, and tablets.

▶ **Endpoint detection and response.** This is a comprehensive endpoint security tool that combines real-time continuous monitoring and data collecting on endpoints with the capabilities of rules-based automated response and analysis.

▶ **Comprehensive data security platform.** It protects sensitive data under multiple IT environments, including multi-cloud and hybrid. Not only can data security platforms provide backups and encryption, but they can also alert IT professionals to data vulnerabilities and threats automatically and in real time before data breaches. Additionally, they can assist in meeting regulatory compliance requirements.

▶ **File integrity monitoring (FIM).** FIM is an IT security process and technology that validates the integrity of operating system, database, and application software files by way of comparing the present file state to a known, good baseline. If FIM identifies that files have been modified, or corrupted, it can issue warnings for further investigation and, if necessary, perform remediation. FIM encompasses both proactive, rules-based surveillance and reactive inspection.

▶ **Intrusion detection system (IDS) and intrusion prevention system (IPS).** Both IDS and IPS sift through network traffic in search of abnormal patterns or suspicious activity. The primary distinction between IDS and IPS is that, while IDS will notify you of anomalous flow of data, it will not block or prevent the flow. In comparison, IPS incorporate firewall-like functions to make proactive adjustments to restrict certain suspicious traffic and deny it as swiftly as possible. Both solutions largely rely on signatures to recognize traffic patterns that are similar to known attack tactics. This means that they may be ineffective against emerging threats if a signature for the assault has not yet been recognized.

▶ **Unified threat management.** This type of system integrates a range of security functions such as anti-virus, firewalls, and IDS and IPS into a single platform or device. By unifying all or some of these tools, overall threat management can be simplified. However, this may produce single point of failure and may not deliver best-of-breed solution for each of its components.

▶ **Security information and event management (SIEM).** An SIEM solution—working alongside with firewall, anti-virus, and IDS and IPS—collects and correlates data from those systems as well as log and event data generated by servers and applications. SIEM technology simplifies the process of reviewing and analyzing data from various systems in order to gain more complete understanding on an organization's security condition. SIEM can prioritize and automate cyber threat responses in accordance with a firm's risk management policies. Today's SIEM solutions incorporate advanced detection techniques such as user behavior analytics and AI. Additionally, many firms are combining their SIEMs with security orchestration, automation, and response platforms, which further automate and speed up the response to cyber incidents without human intervention.

▶ **Sandboxing.** It is a technique of creating an isolated test environment, a "sandbox," in which to run a suspicious file or URL included in an email and then observe the results. If the file or URL exhibits malicious activity, then it indicates a new threat. The sandbox must be a secure, virtual environment that precisely mirrors production servers. Sandboxing is particularly useful against zero-day threats.

Cybersecurity Trends

In terms of cyberattacks, the landscape of cyber warfare has shifted substantially as a result of the COVID-19 pandemic. Increased interactions with customers via digital channels and unexpected, pandemic-driven remote work setups introduced a large number of new vectors for cyberattacks. Cloud-based infrastructure and widely available attacker tools (PowerShell, Mimi Katz, and Cobalt Strike, applications all developed for legitimate use), combined with anonymous payment via Bitcoin, are tilting the playing field and empowering threat actors of all sizes.[44] In addition, cyber threats are becoming more and more sophisticated as a result of the availability of emerging technologies such as AI and machine learning, and the growing collaboration among hacktivists including state actors.

According to Check Point Software Technologies' *Cyber Attack Trends Mid-Year Report 2021*, a global increase in cyberattacks was witnessed in the first half of 2021. US firms experienced an average of 443 weekly attacks by the middle of 2021, a 17% rise since the beginning of the same year. In Europe, the Middle East, and Africa, the average weekly number of attacks per firm was 777 in the middle of 2021, an increase of 36% since the start of the year. Weekly attacks against organizations in Asia and the Pacific totaled 1,338 mid-2021, reflecting a 13% rise during the review period. There was a huge global surge of 93% in the number of ransomware attacks. Ransomware actors have adopted a new strategy that adds a third step to the double extortion technique: in addition to stealing sensitive data from organizations and threatening to publicly release it unless a ransom is paid, attackers are now targeting organizations' customers or business partners for ransom as well.

In terms of cybersecurity strategy, the rise in location independence in business driven by the COVID-19 pandemic and the increased use of distributed cloud services have caused security professionals to experience widespread disruption, particularly in IAM solutions, and compelled businesses to embrace distributed architectural approaches in cybersecurity. Gartner defined this approach as the so-called "cybersecurity mesh," which allows scalable and reliable cyber management by shifting the focus away from conventional IT perimeter protection and toward a more modular approach that centralizes policy orchestration but decentralizes policy enforcement. The cybersecurity mesh is a critical component of a "zero-trust" network security strategy, in which any device is presumed to be untrustworthy when accessing the broader network. The mesh architecture ensures that all data, systems, and equipment are treated equally and securely regardless of their location within or outside the network. By default, any connection used to access data is considered unreliable until the security protocol validates that it is, in fact, reliable. Gartner predicts that cybersecurity mesh will support more than half of all IAM requests by 2025. In addition, as businesses migrate their data to the cloud and modernize their IT infrastructure, concerns over data vulnerabilities grow, resulting in high demand for security services. The global security-as-a-service market was valued at approximately USD9.2 billion in 2020. It is projected to reach more than USD22 billion in 2026.[45] In 2020, more than 80% of respondents from a global survey stated that the consumption of security as a service, secure cloud migration, and the implementation of zero-trust architecture, among other things, are their organizations' post-pandemic cybersecurity priorities (Figure 19).

From a technological standpoint, as the business environment becomes more complicated and digital transformation accelerates, the need for hyper-automation in cybersecurity also increases. Organizations

---

44   Sonicwall. 2021. *Cyber Threat Report*. p. 7. https://www.sonicwall.com/2022-cyber-threat-report/.

45   Mordor   Intelligence.   https://www.mordorintelligence.com/industry-reports/security-as-a-service-market;   Statista.   2021. https://www.statista.com/statistics/595164/worldwide-security-as-a-service-market-size/.

are seeking the assistance of optimized and connected technologies. Since digital commerce requires efficiency and speed, anything that is automatable should be automated. According to SANS Institute's *2020 Automation and Integration Survey*, the most widely used tools for security automation include IPS, IDS, and unified threat management alerts; SIEM analysis; endpoint detection and response capabilities; vulnerability management; log analysis; and identity management (Figure 20). As Figure 8 also showed, in the finance sector, AI is most widely used for fraud detection and other cybersecurity issues.

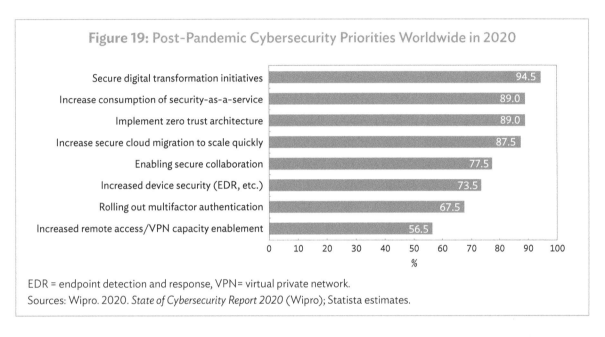

Figure 19: Post-Pandemic Cybersecurity Priorities Worldwide in 2020

EDR = endpoint detection and response, VPN= virtual private network.
Sources: Wipro. 2020. *State of Cybersecurity Report 2020* (Wipro); Statista estimates.

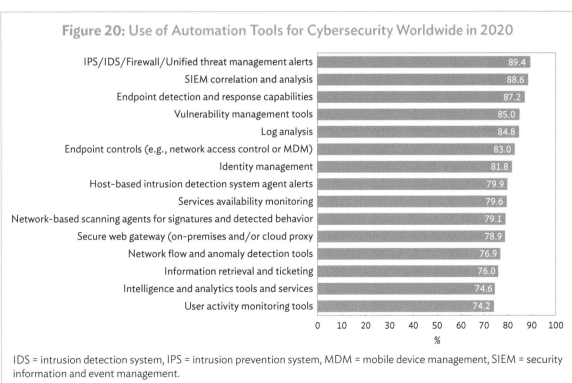

Figure 20: Use of Automation Tools for Cybersecurity Worldwide in 2020

IDS = intrusion detection system, IPS = intrusion prevention system, MDM = mobile device management, SIEM = security information and event management.
Sources: Adapted from SANS Institute. 2020. *SANS Automation and Integration Survey*.

6.   (Open) Application Programming Interfaces

Basic Concept

An API is a collection of instructions that define how one application communicates and interacts with another. An API can be used by both internal developers within the organization that established it and external developers. In other words, an API might be tailored to a specific pair of systems, or it can be a shared standard that enables interoperability across multiple systems. In contrast to a user interface, which links a computer to a human, an API connects computers or software applications to other computers or software applications. An API is composed of parts of the whole system that serve as tools or services available to the developer. One main purpose of APIs is to conceal the internal structures of a system, revealing only the portions that a developer would find useful and ensuring that they remain consistent even if the internal details change later. APIs are commonly used to refer to web APIs, which enable communication between computers connected via the internet.

One of the most significant advantages of APIs is that they provide powerful resources for rapid development. Instead of designing solutions from scratch, developers can simply apply existing functionality via APIs. Also, the API provides a robust and versatile mechanism for connecting various software applications. APIs enable the integration and interoperability of a diverse set of independent software applications. Through better connectivity and collaboration enabled by APIs, organizations can design interoperable components that optimize operations and empower enterprises to deliver required functionality with minimum constraints. Further, APIs hold tremendous potential for disruptive innovation. APIs support businesses to make the most of the advanced capabilities of technological behemoths with fewer resources, quickly adapt to changing customer needs, and explore new growth opportunities.

Types of Application Programming Interfaces

APIs are widely used and acknowledged in web applications. Therefore, the term "APIs" is frequently used interchangeably with "web APIs." There are four distinct types of APIs that are commonly used in web-based applications, depending on their intended scope of use:

▶ **Public or Open APIs.** Public APIs are accessible to and usable by any third-party developer or business. They may be totally open or need registration and the use of an API key. A business that develops a business strategy centered on sharing its applications and data with other businesses can create and deploy a public API.

▶ **Private or Internal APIs.** Private APIs are intended for use exclusively within the organization to connect systems and data. They allow separate teams or divisions of an organization to utilize the resources and data of one another. Private APIs offer various benefits over conventional integration approaches, including enhanced security and access control, a centralized audit log of system access, and a standardized interface for linking different applications.

▶ **Partner APIs.** Technically, partner APIs are comparable to open APIs, but they have restricted access normally controlled via a third-party API gateway. They are typically created with a specific purpose, such as granting access to a paid service. This type of API is very common in the SAAS ecosystem.

- ▶ **Composite APIs.** Composite APIs are used to create a sequence of connected or interdependent processes by combining two or more APIs. Composite APIs are particularly advantageous in microservice architectures, where users may require data from multiple services to accomplish a single operation.[46] Composite APIs can help minimize server load and enhance application functionality by returning all the data a user requires in a single call.[47]

Application Programming Interface Architectures and Protocols

APIs for web services facilitate the transmission of commands and data between disparate computing infrastructures connected via the internet. This necessitates the use of unambiguous, standardized communication protocols and architectures that interact seamlessly with one another. The term "standardized protocols and architectures" refers to the capacity of disparate systems to communicate with one another and to the usage of diverse programming languages or technologies. The following are the most common types of API protocols or architectures:

- ▶ **Representational state transfer (REST).** REST is likely the most widely used approach for developing APIs. Unlike the other web service APIs, it is not a protocol; rather, it is a set of architectural formulas. To begin, REST APIs, usually termed "RESTful APIs," are based on a client or server architecture that separates the front and back ends of the API, allowing for greater development and implementation liberty. Second, they are "stateless," which implies that the server APIs do not maintain any client data or status information between requests. Third, they allow caching, which grants APIs to save responses. Lastly, they can communicate directly or via intermediary systems such as API gateways.

- ▶ **Remote procedural call (RPC).** The RPC protocol offers a simple means of transmitting multiple parameters and receiving results. While REST APIs are mostly used to share data or resources such as documents, RPC APIs trigger executable actions or processes. RPC can be coded in one of two different programming languages, JSON or XML; these APIs are referred to as JSON-RPC and XML-RPC, respectively.

- ▶ **Simple object access protocol (SOAP).** SOAP is a communication protocol defined by the World Wide Web Consortium. It is widely used to establish web service APIs, which are typically written in XML. SOAP is compatible with a variety of internet-based communication protocols, including HTTP, SMTP, and TCP. Also, since SOAP is extendable and style-neutral, programmers can create SOAP APIs in a number of ways and easily add features. The SOAP approach outlines the processing of SOAP messages, the features and modules that are included, the communication protocol(s) that are supported, and the SOAP message structure. In comparison to REST's flexibility, SOAP is a highly structured, strictly managed, and well-defined standard.

Apart from APIs based on the aforementioned architectures and protocols, many financial market participants—including investment banks, prime brokers, and asset management firms—utilize a

---

[46] Microservices are scalable, compact, componentized software services with a limited scope that can be combined with other services to build complete applications. The term "microservice architecture" refers to the process of designing, developing, and running complicated, multifunction software as a collection of smaller autonomous services. Microservices design maintains service independence by separating each function of an application into a distinct service that can be implemented and updated independently.

[47] An API call is a client-made request to an API. After then, the API will return with the response data.

Financial Information eXchange (FIX) API, which is based on the FIX protocol, a vendor-neutral electronic communication protocol for the real-time exchange of securities transaction information. The FIX API is primarily used by those who already have FIX-capable software.

Application Programming Interface-Powered Digital Transformation

Digital transformation, propelled by the COVID-19 pandemic and shifting market conditions, is heavily reliant on an organization's capacity to bundle its services and resources into reusable software modules. To realize this value, however, it must be released from silos and made interoperable and reusable in a variety of contexts including through the combination of its internal assets with assets of external counterparties. APIs facilitate these symbioses by enabling programmers to quickly access and integrate digital resources stored in disparate infrastructures. While the application scenarios for APIs are virtually limitless, there are few noteworthy areas.

Increased SAAS use and hybrid cloud adoption by businesses enable API deployments. Global cloud spending on cloud services (e.g., IAAS, PAAS, and SAAS) has been expanding at a notable pace since 2016, with SAAS spending accounting for the lion's share (Figure 12). Additionally, the hybrid cloud model, which combines two or more cloud types (i.e., public, private, or community), has been the most commonly used manner of cloud implementation (Figure 15). The growth of SAAS and hybrid cloud-based APIs highlights the crucial nature of development elasticity.

APIs are crucial components of microservice architectures and DevOps.[48] Certain APIs are used to share cloud-native microservices. These microservices provide very flexible, granular, and modular development methodologies, enabling an application with microservices to evolve with time. Similarly, as API programs become more specialized, DevOps, or the automation of development processes, has attracted increased attention and investment in enterprises as a means of expediting the deployment of new products and services. Many organizations begin their DevOps journey by implementing technology that enables development teams to eliminate inefficiency throughout the software development process. A common step is to expose assets with business value and to construct continuous integration processes that span the design, development, and testing phases, utilizing a range of APIs.

In the finance sector, service systems are becoming increasingly "API-powered," with smaller FinTech startups and more established financial institutions cooperating to upgrade their offerings. To begin, open banking, which emerged in Europe in 2015, offers third-party financial service providers access to customer banking, transaction, and other financial data from banks via APIs. Second, as technology-driven business models evolve to make finance more approachable, marketable, and competitive through data connectivity and analysis, the principle of open banking is advancing into open finance, which empowers users to share their financial information—regardless of its origin—with third parties via APIs to gain access to new products and services personalized to their unique needs.[49] Third, in a similar

---

[48] DevOps is a set of techniques that integrate software development (Dev) with information technology operations (Ops), with the goal of shortening the systems development life cycle with minimal disruption and ensuring continuous provision of highly reliable software quality.

[49] As transactions can easily cross borders, financial institutions and service providers are also faced with compliance issues not just within the jurisdiction they are registered or licensed but also with other jurisdictions in which their transactions will touch base. Thus, there is the possibility of adopting an open structure for classifying licensing-related requirements and other regulatory content across various jurisdictions to assist the ease of compliance or vetting of participants prior to being permitted to participate in an open finance ecosystem.

context, an increasing number of nonbank companies are embracing embedded finance—banking-like financial services such as bank accounts or wallets, payments, and lending offered by nonbanks—to keep customers or enhance customer experience and value. To accommodate the growing demand for embedded finance, banks are increasingly offering banking as a service—bundled offers, frequently white-labeled or co-branded—that nonbanks can employ to serve their customers. So, banks may scale banking as a service more quickly with process automation and APIs, putting embedded finance within reach of more nonbank companies.

APIs have become vital to every enterprise, but their widespread adoption makes them a tempting target for threat actors. Access control and rate limiting restrictions alone cannot counter today's sophisticated attacks.[50] AI is establishing itself as a critical component of enterprises' API management and security operations. AI can assist organizations in predicting and modeling API behavior, detecting abnormalities in real-time, identifying security issues fast, accurately diagnosing the root cause of security and performance warnings, and reducing response time. This technology can also assist in ensuring that APIs comply with security and compliance standards and keep sensitive data from being abused internally.

---

[50] The rate limit, alternatively called the API limit, is the maximum number of API requests that an application or user can perform in a given time. If this limit is exceeded, the application or user may be throttled. API requests submitted by a throttled user or application will be denied. Rate limiting is critical for API security, as denial-of-service attacks can bring a server to a halt with an overwhelming number of API calls.

New Technologies in ASEAN+3 Financial Market Infrastructure

A. Overview

This chapter describes the extent to which FMIs in the ASEAN+3 region are applying the six new technologies mentioned in the previous chapter—DLT, AI, bid data analytics, cloud computing, cybersecurity, and API—to their systems and services. The new technology stocktaking in this chapter is mainly based on a survey, conducted in April–July 2021, of CSDs and central banks in the ASEAN+3 region that are members of the Cross-Border Settlement Infrastructure Forum (CSIF).[51]

The survey questionnaire mainly comprised the following (while there were also some miscellaneous questions as shown in Appendix 1):

▶ Do the CSIF member institutions have systems that apply any of the six new technologies applied; the names of these systems; their levels of application such as proof of concept (POC), prototype, pilot, and production;[52] and an overview on those systems with new technologies and their development history?

▶ Do the members have plans to apply any of those new technologies to their systems in the future?

▶ Have the central banks issued a CBDC or have a plan to issue in the near future?

The survey result are summarized below:[53]

▶ Overall, 20 of the 25 CSIF member institutions responded to the survey.[54] Of the respondents, 16 of the 20 institutions (80%) stated that they have explored, or are currently exploring, at least one of the six selected new technologies: five member institutions have explored a single new technology; three have explored two; six have explored three; and two have explored four. If we divide the total number of responses into central banks and CSDs, we find that 9 of the 12 central banks (75%) and 7 of the 8 CSDs (88%) have applied at least one of the six new technologies (Figure 21).

---

[51] CSIF membership in the ASEAN+3 region comprises 12 CSDs and 13 central banks. The CSIF falls under the ambit of the Asian Bond Markets Initiative (ABMI).

[52] A POC is a small activity designed to evaluate the real-world viability of a vague concept or idea. This is not about delivering the idea, but about showing its feasibility. A prototype is the visible and practical embodiment of an idea that simulates the entire system or a significant portion. While a POC demonstrates whether a concept or idea can be implemented, a prototype illustrates how it will be implemented. Prototypes should be used when there is an idea about a solution but no certainty about how it will work. Results from prototyping can then be used to refine the concept. A pilot is a productionized version of a system offered to a subset of the entire audience. The purpose of a pilot study is to obtain a deeper understanding of how the product will be serviced in the actual domain and to optimize it.

[53] After the CSIF members responded to the survey, ADB gathered additional necessary information through a series of written questions and answers and online meetings with individual member organizations.

[54] The 20 survey respondents comprised 8 CSDs and 12 central banks: 8 out of 12 CSDs (67%) and 12 out of 13 central banks (92%) among all CSIF members.

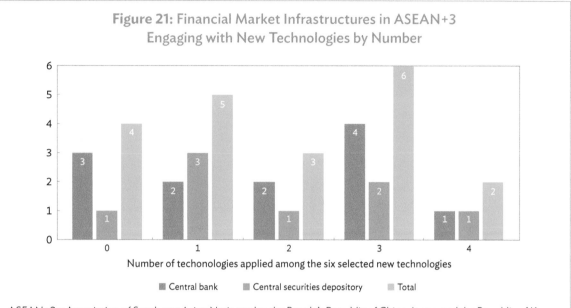

Figure 21: Financial Market Infrastructures in ASEAN+3
Engaging with New Technologies by Number

Number of techonologies applied among the six selected new technologies

■ Central bank   ■ Central securities depository   ■ Total

ASEAN+3 = Association of Southeast Asian Nations plus the People's Republic of China, Japan, and the Republic of Korea.
Notes: 20 out of 25 Cross-Border Settlement Infrastructure Forum member institutions responded to the survey.
Source: ABMI 2021 CSIF member survey.

▶ In terms of the number of the CSIF member institutions working with the new technologies, six out of 20 institutions that replied to the survey indicated that they have engaged in, or are currently involved in, DLT: 3 institutions with AI, 5 institutions with big data analytics, 2 institutions with cloud computing, 8 institutions with new cybersecurity technologies, and 10 institutions with (open) APIs. Among the six new technologies that CSIF members have attempted or are attempting to use, the top three new technologies that the members are trying to apply actively are DLT, cybersecurity technology, and (open) APIs. Each of these involved at least six member institutions, accounting for 30% of the respondents. Central banks and CSDs in the ASEAN+3 region tend to be less interested in AI and cloud computing technology (Figure 22).

▶ The survey discovered a total of 38 application cases for the six new technologies among CSIF member institutions: 22 cases from central banks and 16 from CSDs. (Open) API application cases accounted for 26% of all cases (10 out of 38 cases), followed by DLT and cybersecurity, each of which accounted for 21% (8 out of 38 cases). All eight cybersecurity application cases were at the production level of application. In comparison, the other technologies had multiple levels of application: the eight DLT application cases included two POCs, one prototype, two pilots, and three productions; the six big data analytics application cases include one POC, one pilots, and four productions; the 10 (open) API application cases included two POCs, one prototype, and seven productions; and the like. There are cases of the production stage of application for all six technologies (Figure 23 and Figure 30).

▶ Figure 24 shows the number of FMI systems with new technologies applied from a different angle by the number of each application level. Production cases accounted for 24 of the 38 total cases, or 63%, given that the majority of application cases involving cybersecurity and (open) APIs were at the production level. The survey also identified that CSIF members are exploring

DLT at all application levels, and there are three production-level DLT-based systems in the ASEAN+3 region.

▶ Concerning the central banks' systems, the survey identified 22 systems that employed one of the six new technologies. Similarly, (open) API application cases made for the largest portion of all cases, accounting for 32%, followed by DLT and cybersecurity, which accounted for 18% (Figure 25), and production-level systems, which accounted for 59% (Figure 26).

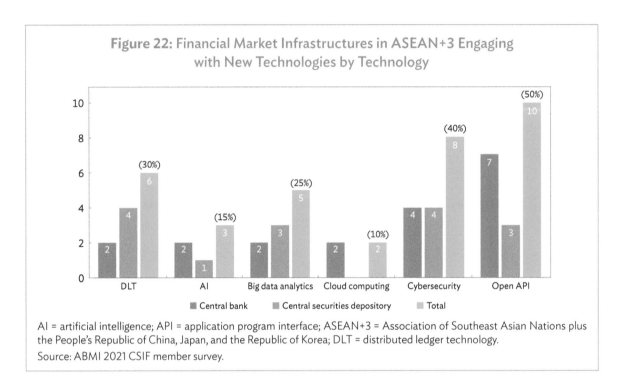

Figure 22: Financial Market Infrastructures in ASEAN+3 Engaging with New Technologies by Technology

AI = artificial intelligence; API = application program interface; ASEAN+3 = Association of Southeast Asian Nations plus the People's Republic of China, Japan, and the Republic of Korea; DLT = distributed ledger technology.
Source: ABMI 2021 CSIF member survey.

Figure 23: Financial Market Infrastructure Systems with New Technologies by Technology

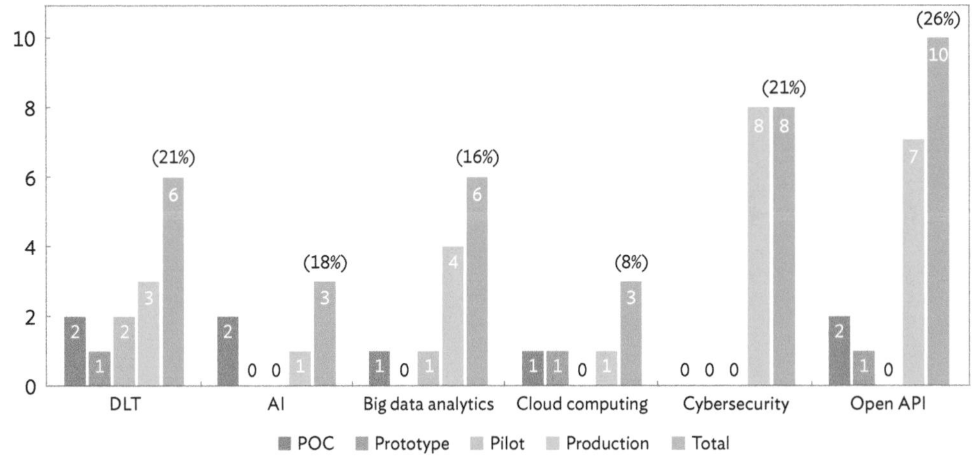

AI = artificial intelligence, API = application program interface, DLT = distributed ledger technology, POC = proof of concept.
Source: ABMI 2021 CSIF member survey.

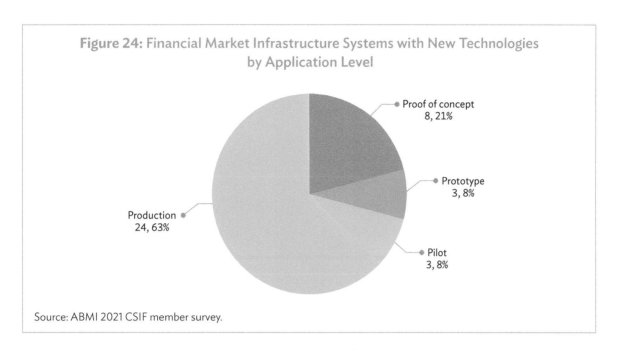

Figure 24: Financial Market Infrastructure Systems with New Technologies by Application Level

Source: ABMI 2021 CSIF member survey.

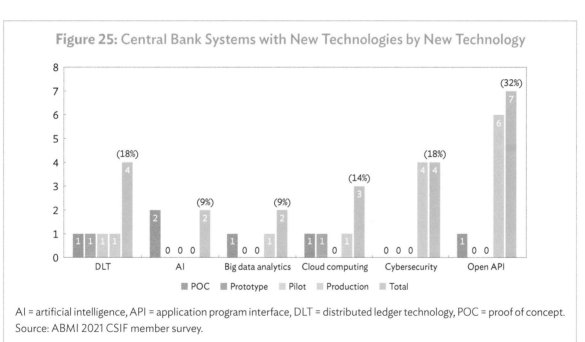

Figure 25: Central Bank Systems with New Technologies by New Technology

AI = artificial intelligence, API = application program interface, DLT = distributed ledger technology, POC = proof of concept.
Source: ABMI 2021 CSIF member survey.

▶ In the case of CSDs' systems, application cases for DLT, big data analytics, and cybersecurity accounted for the largest share, accounting for 25% each, while there was no application case for cloud computing in CSD systems (Figure 27). The majority of CSD systems' application cases were also at the production level (Figure 28).

Figure 29 shows the application cases of CSIF member organizations that responded to the survey by application level. Figure 30 combines these cases by technology.

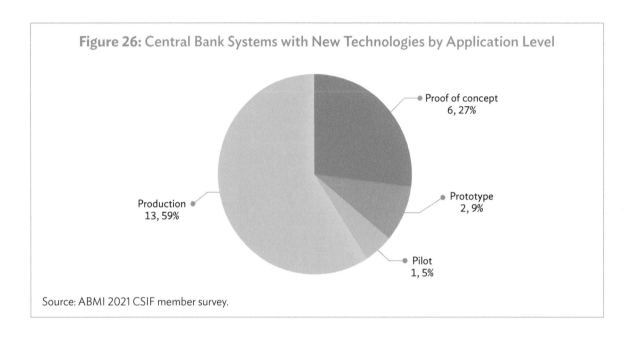

Figure 26: Central Bank Systems with New Technologies by Application Level

Proof of concept
6, 27%

Prototype
2, 9%

Pilot
1, 5%

Production
13, 59%

Source: ABMI 2021 CSIF member survey.

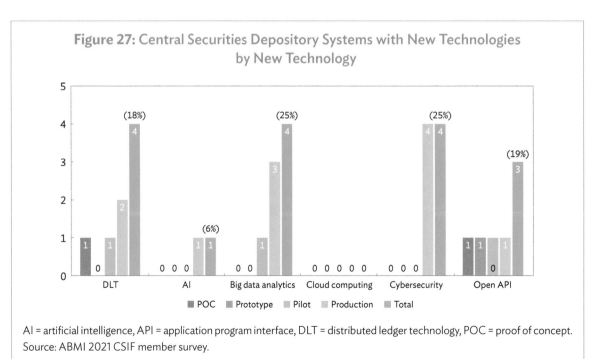

Figure 27: Central Securities Depository Systems with New Technologies by New Technology

AI = artificial intelligence, API = application program interface, DLT = distributed ledger technology, POC = proof of concept.
Source: ABMI 2021 CSIF member survey.

NEW TECHNOLOGIES IN ASEAN+3 FINANCIAL MARKET INFRASTRUCTURE

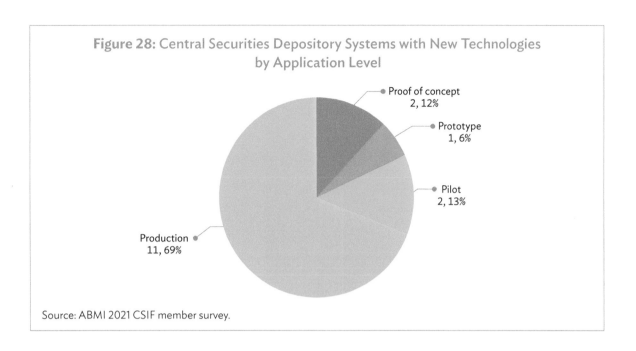

Figure 28: Central Securities Depository Systems with New Technologies by Application Level

Proof of concept
2, 12%

Prototype
1, 6%

Pilot
2, 13%

Production
11, 69%

Source: ABMI 2021 CSIF member survey.

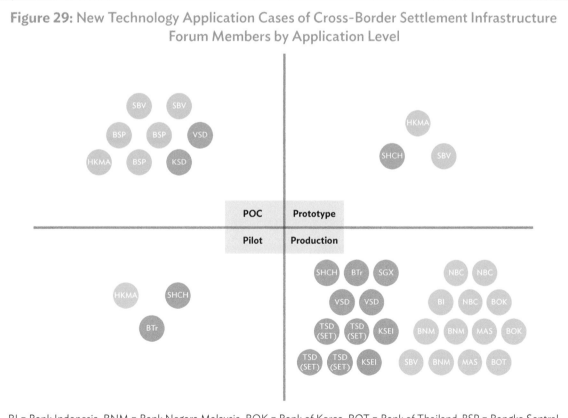

Figure 29: New Technology Application Cases of Cross-Border Settlement Infrastructure Forum Members by Application Level

BI = Bank Indonesia, BNM = Bank Negara Malaysia, BOK = Bank of Korea, BOT = Bank of Thailand, BSP = Bangko Sentral ng Pilipinas, BTr = Bureau of Treasury, HKMA = Hong Kong Monetary Authority, KSD = Korea Securities Depository, KSEI = PT Kustodian Sentral Efek Indonesia, MAS = Monetary Authority of Singapore, NBC = National Bank of Cambodia, POC = proof of concept, SBV = State Bank of Vietnam, SET = Stock Exchange of Thailand, SGX = Singapore Exchange, SHCH = Shanghai Clearing House, TSD = Thailand Securities Depository, VSD = Vietnam Securities Depository.

Legend: ● central bank; and ● central securities depository.

Source: 2021 ABMI CSIF member survey.

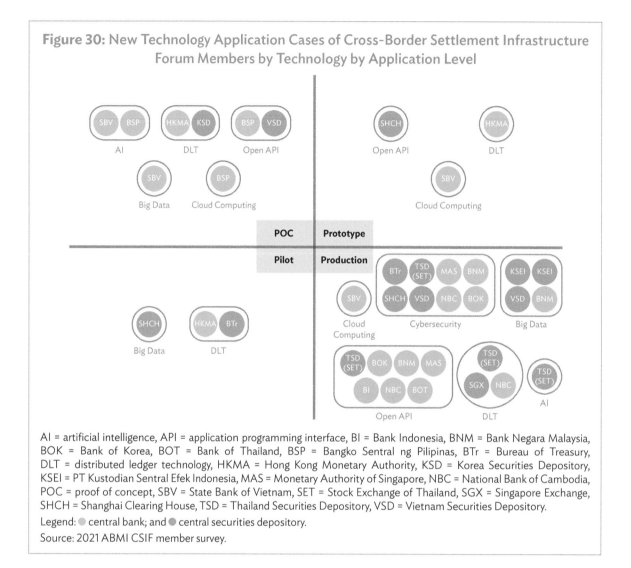

Figure 30: New Technology Application Cases of Cross-Border Settlement Infrastructure Forum Members by Technology by Application Level

AI = artificial intelligence, API = application programming interface, BI = Bank Indonesia, BNM = Bank Negara Malaysia, BOK = Bank of Korea, BOT = Bank of Thailand, BSP = Bangko Sentral ng Pilipinas, BTr = Bureau of Treasury, DLT = distributed ledger technology, HKMA = Hong Kong Monetary Authority, KSD = Korea Securities Depository, KSEI = PT Kustodian Sentral Efek Indonesia, MAS = Monetary Authority of Singapore, NBC = National Bank of Cambodia, POC = proof of concept, SBV = State Bank of Vietnam, SET = Stock Exchange of Thailand, SGX = Singapore Exchange, SHCH = Shanghai Clearing House, TSD = Thailand Securities Depository, VSD = Vietnam Securities Depository.
Legend: ● central bank; and ● central securities depository.
Source: 2021 ABMI CSIF member survey.

The following six sections will cover the individual systems to which each CSIF member institution has applied, or is applying, one or more of the six new technologies.[55]

B. Distributed Ledger (Blockchain) Technology

1. Distributed Ledger Technology-Based Systems

As described in previous section, six of the 20 CSIF member institutions that responded to the survey, two central banks and four CSDs, have engaged in or currently engaged in DLT, and there are eight application cases including two POCs, one prototype, two pilots, and three production cases. The Hong Kong Monetary Authority (HKMA), the central banking institution of Hong Kong, China, has

---

[55] Responses from CSIF members regarding their cross-border services that are not directly related to the six key technologies can be found in Appendix 2.

three DLT application cases: one POC, one prototype development, and one pilot. Cambodia's central bank, the National Bank of Cambodia (NBC), has one production-level application case. For CSDs, Korea Securities Depository (KSD) has one POC case; the Bureau of the Treasury (BTr), which serves as the CSD for Philippine government bonds, has one pilot case; and Thailand Securities Depository (TSD) and Singapore Exchange (SGX), which operates the Central Depository (Pte.) Limited (CDP), Singapore's CSD, each have one production-level application case (Figure 31).

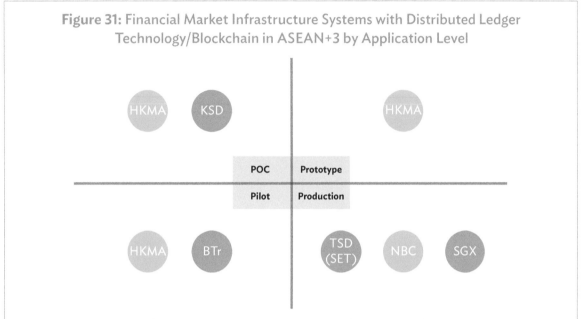

Figure 31: Financial Market Infrastructure Systems with Distributed Ledger Technology/Blockchain in ASEAN+3 by Application Level

ASEAN+3 = Association of Southeast Asian Nations plus the People's Republic of China, Japan, and the Republic of Korea; BTr = Bureau of Treasury; HKMA = Hong Kong Monetary Authority; KSD = Korea Securities Depository; NBC = National Bank of Cambodia; POC = proof of concept; SET = Stock Exchange of Thailand; SGX = Singapore Exchange; TSD = Thailand Securities Depository.

Legend: ● central bank; and ● central securities depository.

Source: 2021 ABMI CSIF member survey.

HKMA has experimented, or is experimenting, with DLT on its CBDC projects and also to support the streamlining of the processes of trade finance and small and medium-sized enterprise (SME) financing.[56] NBC launched a blockchain-powered retail payment system in 2020 to address the issue of interconnectivity and interoperability across multiple platforms of domestic payment operators, to promote financial inclusion, and to expedite Khmer riel cash payment. All four CSDs in the region are leveraging DLT in the field of security issuing to enhance efficiency by reducing process time, cost and risks. Table 8 outlines the DLT-based systems of the six CSIF member institutions.

Boxes 1 and 2 highlight NBC's Bakong payment system and TSD's scripless government bond issuance system. The next subsection will examine in depth various CBDC projects of the region's central banks.

---

[56] HKMA was the only central bank in the region that responded to the survey with information about its CBDC projects. Given that many more central banks in the region are experimenting with CBDCs, the number of central banks experimenting with DLT may be greater. CBDC projects in the region will be explained in further detail later in this report.

Table 8: Financial Market Infrastructure Systems with Distributed
Ledger Technology in ASEAN+3

	Institution	System	App. Level	Period	Description
CB	HKMA	eTradeConnect	Pilot	• Started in 2017	• A blockchain-based trade finance platform developed by a consortium of 12 major banks in Hong Kong, China with the facilitation of HKMA.
				• A pilot system launched in Oct 2018	• The system aims to digitize paper-based documents automate the trade finance process to reduce errors and risks of fraud.
		CBDC projects	Prototype	• 2017 • 2019 • Started in 2021	• Project LionRock (HKMA) • Project Inthanon-LionRock (HKMA and BOT) • mCBDC project (HKMA, BOT, DCI of PBOC, CBUAE, and BIS IH)
		Commercial Data Interchange (CDI)	POC	• POC phase 1: 2020 • POC phase 2: 2021 • Production to be launched in 2023	• CDI is a consent-based financial infrastructure enabling more secure and efficient data flow between banks and commercial firms, particularly SMEs, to solve long-standing pain points in SME financing. • CDI allows SMEs to use their own trade-related and other commercial data to facilitate trade finance application process (POC phase 1) and alternative credit scoring conducted by banks (POC phase 2).
	NBC	Bakong payment system (Project Bakong)	Production	• Started in 2016 • Launched in Oct 2020	• A blockchain-based national retail payment system • Prefunded for settlement (a synthetic CBDC) • Built on Hyperledger Iroha, an open source blockchain framework implementation under Hyperledger Projects • Total of 1.7M transactions from July 2019 to June 2021 (USD0.42 billion + KHR443.8 billion)
CSD	BTr	Bonds.PH (Mobile application)	Pilot	• A pilot system launched in Jul 2020	• A DLT-based retail primary offering facility of government bonds, which allows investors to place subscriptions in retail bonds during the primary offering • Partnering with UnionBank, a government securities eligible dealer, and Philippine Digital Asset Exchange

continued on next page

Table 8 *continued*

Institution	System	App. Level	Period	Description
KSD	Crowdfunding platform	POC	• Q1–Q3 2021	• DLT-based security token offering a platform for crowdfunding[a, b] • POC successfully completed at the end of September 2021
TSD (SET)	Scripless govt. bond issuance system ("DLT Scripless Bond Project")	Production	• POC: Q1–Q3 2018 • Production: Started in Q4 2018 and launched in Jun 2020	• A DLT-based retail scripless government savings bond issuance system • Built with Hyperledger Fabric, another open source blockchain framework under Hyperledger Projects • As of May 2021, seven government bonds had been issued through the system.
SGX	"Marketnode" Issuer platform	Production	• Pilot: Completed in Aug 2020 • Production: launched in Jan 2021	• A DLT-based fixed-income digital asset issuance platform • Focusing on automation of end-to-end issuance, deposit, and post-trade asset servicing with smart contracts • Developed via a joint venture between SGX and Temasek

ASEAN+3 = Association of Southeast Asian Nations plus the People's Republic of China, Japan, and the Republic of Korea; BIS IH = Bank for International Settlements Innovation Hub; BOT = the Bank of Thailand; BTr = Bureau of Treasury; CB = central bank; CBDC = central bank digital currency; CBUAE = the Central Bank of the United Arab Emirates; CSD = central securities depository; DCI of PBOC = Digital Currency Institute of the People's Bank of China; DLT = distributed ledger technology; HKMA = Hong Kong Monetary Authority; KSD = Korea Securities Depository; NBC = National Bank of Cambodia; POC = proof of concept; Q1 = first quarter; Q3 = third quarter; Q4 = fourth quarter; SET = Stock Exchange of Thailand; SGX = Singapore Exchange; SMEs = small and medium-sized enterprises; TSD = Thailand Securities Depository.

[a] A security token offering is the process whereby a financial security (or a digital representation of a financial security) is issued in the form of a digital asset; typically, the digital asset represents ownership rights in an underlying company and/or its assets. This is entirely different to the initial coin offering, which are "utility tokens"—i.e., digital tokens that provide access to a future product/service but do not entitle the holder to ownership of an asset or equity. Deloitte. 2019. *Are Token Assets the Securities of Tomorrow?* https://www2.deloitte.com/lu/en/pages/technology/articles/are-token-assets-securities-tomorrow.html.

[b] Crowdfunding is the practice of soliciting modest sums of funds from a large number of individuals in order to finance a new business. Crowdfunding leverages the widespread availability of enormous networks of people via social media and crowdfunding platforms to connect investors and entrepreneurs, which can boost entrepreneurship by broadening the pool of capital investments beyond the conventional sphere of the owners and private investors.

Sources: ABMI 2021 CSIF Member Survey and websites of each institution.

Box 1: National Bank of Cambodia's Bakong Payment System (Project Bakong)

The journey of Project Bakong started in 2016 with the forming a working group to explore the use of blockchain and DLT in payment systems. From 2017 to 2018, the group had developed prototypes and fine-tuned business processes testing and evaluating the prototypes. After going through the pilot testing process in 2019, the Bakong payment system ("Bakong") was officially launched on 28 October 2020.

Bakong is an instant peer-to-peer payment solution connecting all existing banks and multiple domestic payment service providers, so customers can not only use existing infrastructure for fund transfer, but also use a Bakong application to open a Bakong account and transfer money (Figure B1.1).

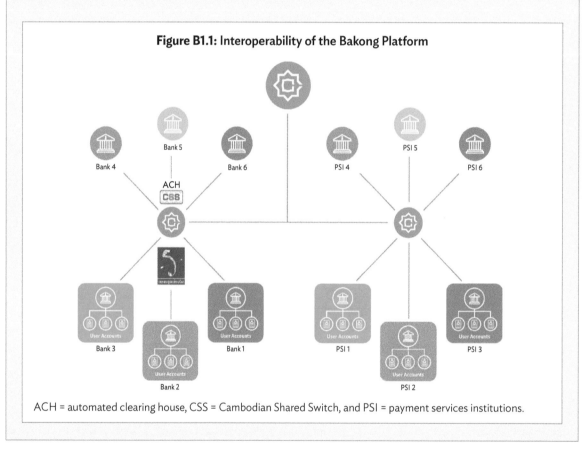

Figure B1.1: Interoperability of the Bakong Platform

ACH = automated clearing house, CSS = Cambodian Shared Switch, and PSI = payment services institutions.

continued on next page

Box 1   *continued*

Bakong can process both Khmer riel and United States dollar transactions, but it requires currency prefunding for settlement. Figures B1.2 and B1.3 illustrate the payment process via Bakong.

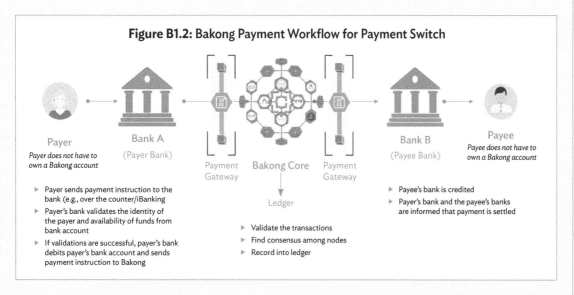

Figure B1.2: Bakong Payment Workflow for Payment Switch

Payer
Payer does not have to own a Bakong account

Bank A
(Payer Bank)

Payment Gateway

Bakong Core

↓

Ledger

Payment Gateway

Bank B
(Payee Bank)

Payee
Payee does not have to own a Bakong account

- ▸ Payer sends payment instruction to the bank (e.g., over the counter/iBanking
- ▸ Payer's bank validates the identity of the payer and availability of funds from bank account
- ▸ If validations are successful, payer's bank debits payer's bank account and sends payment instruction to Bakong

- ▸ Validate the transactions
- ▸ Find consensus among nodes
- ▸ Record into ledger

- ▸ Payee's bank is credited
- ▸ Payer's bank and the payee's banks are informed that payment is settled

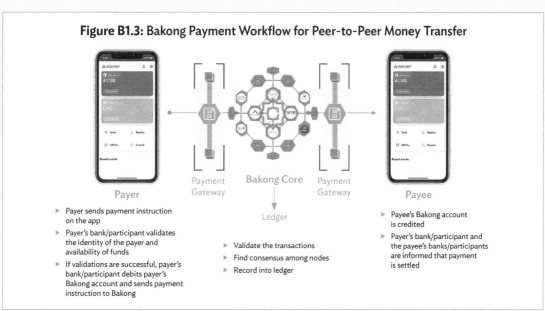

Figure B1.3: Bakong Payment Workflow for Peer-to-Peer Money Transfer

Payer

Payment Gateway

Bakong Core

↓

Ledger

Payment Gateway

Payee

- ▸ Payer sends payment instruction on the app
- ▸ Payer's bank/participant validates the identity of the payer and availability of funds
- ▸ If validations are successful, payer's bank/participant debits payer's Bakong account and sends payment instruction to Bakong

- ▸ Validate the transactions
- ▸ Find consensus among nodes
- ▸ Record into ledger

- ▸ Payee's Bakong account is credited
- ▸ Payer's bank/participant and the payee's banks/participants are informed that payment is settled

Sources: National Bank of Cambodia (NBC). 2020. *Project Bakong: Next Generation Payment System*; and NBC presentation in August 2021 Steering Committee for Capacity Building Webinar.

Box 2: Thailand Securities Depository's Distributed Ledger Technology Scripless Bond Project

The Bank of Thailand (BOT) launched the Distributed Ledger Technology (DLT) Scripless Bond Project in early 2018 to address several deficiencies in the government savings bond sales process, which is based on a non-real-time system, requires duplicate validation steps, and is prone to data errors due to manual reconciliation requirements. Previously, savings bonds were delivered to investors in 15 days (T+15), but this project reduced that time to 2 days (T+2), just like other government bond offerings. The operational enhancements for bond registration and sales are illustrated as below (Figure B2.1).

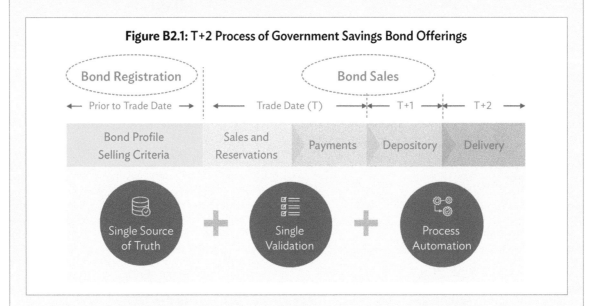

Figure B2.1: T+2 Process of Government Savings Bond Offerings

The platform consists of a public bond channel and a bond agent channel. The public bond channel is primarily used to register bond information. All parties—including the Public Debt Management Office (PDMO), Thailand Seurities Depository (TSD), BOT, and selling agents—have access to the information. The bond agent channel primarily facilitates sales and reservations, account opening, and payment processing between selling agents and BOT, PDMO, and TSD. Access to the information is restricted to those with a need-to-know basis. The DLT platform's architecture, as well as its operational procedures, are schematized in Figure B2.2.

continued on next page

Box 2 *continued*

Figure B2.2: Distributed Ledger Technology Savings Bond Platform

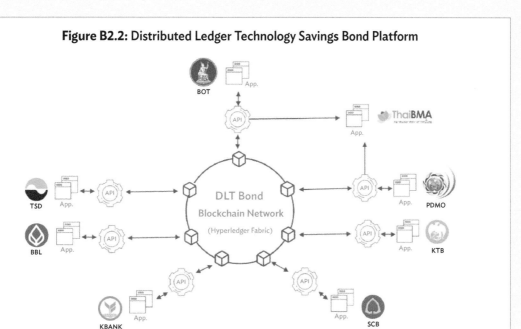

API = application programming interface, App. = application, BBL = Bangkok Bank, BOT = Bank of Thailand, DLT = distributed ledger technology, KBank = Kasikornbank Public Company Limited, KTB = Krungthai Bank Public Company Limited, PDMO = Public Debt Management Office, SCB = Siam Commercial Bank, ThaiBMA = Thai Bond Market Association, TSD = Thailand Securities Depository.

Figure B2.3: Bond Information Registration Process

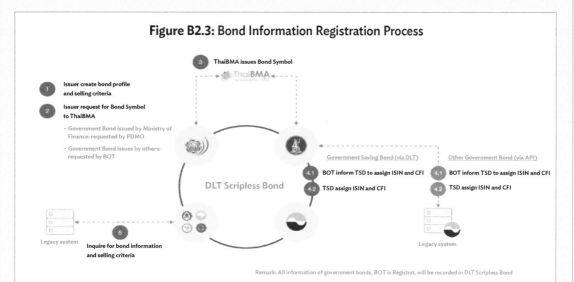

API = application programming interface, BOT = Bank of Thailand, CFI = Classification of Financial Instruments, DLT = distributed ledger technology, ISIN = International Securities Identification Number, PDMO = Public Debt Management Office, ThaiBMA = Thai Bond Mark Association, TSD = Thailand Securities Depository.

continued on next page

Box 2 *continued*

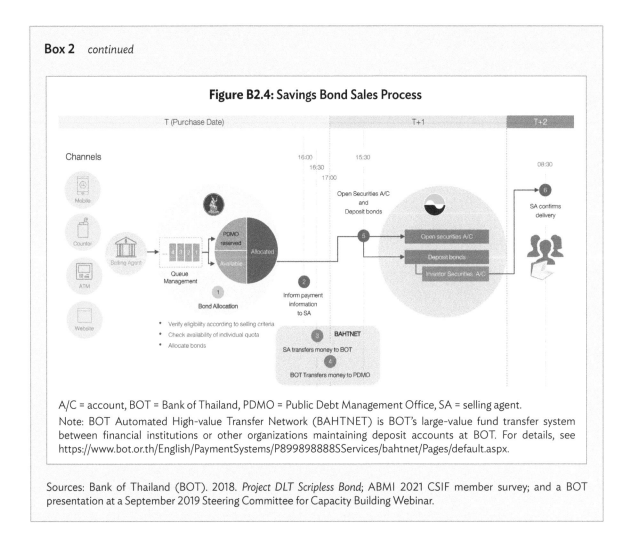

Figure B2.4: Savings Bond Sales Process

A/C = account, BOT = Bank of Thailand, PDMO = Public Debt Management Office, SA = selling agent.

Note: BOT Automated High-value Transfer Network (BAHTNET) is BOT's large-value fund transfer system between financial institutions or other organizations maintaining deposit accounts at BOT. For details, see https://www.bot.or.th/English/PaymentSystems/P899898888SServices/bahtnet/Pages/default.aspx.

Sources: Bank of Thailand (BOT). 2018. *Project DLT Scripless Bond*; ABMI 2021 CSIF member survey; and a BOT presentation at a September 2019 Steering Committee for Capacity Building Webinar.

2.   Central Bank Digital Currency Projects in the ASEAN+3 Region

To date, none of the 14 central banks in the ASEAN+3 region has issued a nationwide CBDC or explicitly stated that it plans to issue a CBDC in the near future. However, as of January 2022, at least 10 central banks in the region were found to be studying CBDCs.

The Bank of Japan (BOJ), the Bank of Thailand (BOT), HKMA, the Monetary Authority of Singapore (MAS), and the People's Bank of China (PBOC) have been actively exploring CBDCs for a reasonably long period of time. Bank Negara Malaysia (BNM) and the Bank of Korea (BOK), on the other hand, have recently embarked on CBDC experiments. In most cases, the scope of the trial expands from wholesale to retail payment as well as from domestic to cross-border financial transactions. In addition, there are instances of a comparative study of DLTs using a variety of DLT solutions available in the DLT platforms market, and it was discovered that CBDC was experimented innovatively to support domestic corporate activities. Notably, there have been approaches to design centralized technical architectures without the use of DLT, while the majority of current CBDC experiments are based on DLT. Table 9 lists the CBDC projects undertaken by the region's central banks.

Table 9: Central Bank Digital Currency Projects in ASEAN+3

Central Bank	App. Level (Project)	Period	Scope of Work	Focus
BI	Research	• Started in 2018	• Conducing comprehensive studies and assessments to see the potential and benefits of CBDS related to conditions in Indonesia	• Still reviewing and assessing CBDC
BOJ (Jointly with ECB)	Experimental research (Project Stella)	• 2017	• Phase 1: Experimental study of large-value payments using DLT (Hyperledger)	• Wholesale CBDC • Domestic PVP
		• 2018	• Phase 2: Experimental study of securities settlement on DLT; three different DLT models (Corda, Elements, and Hyperledger) developed; and both single-ledger DVP and cross-ledger DVP confirmed to be designable	• Domestic DVP; technologies comparison and verification
		• 2019	• Phase 3: Experimental study of cross-border, cross-currency wholesale payment across different ledgers including a distributed ledger (Hyperledger) and a centralized ledger using ILP (Five Bell Ledger)	• Cross-border, cross-currency (bilateral) PVP
		• 2020	• Phase 4: Experimental study of privacy-enhancing technologies on DLT—balancing confidentiality and auditability in a distributed ledger environment	• confidentiality and auditability of DLT
BOJ	POC	• Started in Apr 2021	• Conducting a POC of general purpose CBDC	• Retail CBDC
BOK	Pilot		• Developing a pilot program to examine the technical feasibility of a retail CBDC partnering with a local blockchain solution provider who is also partnering with a global blockchain solution provider (Quorum)	• Retail CBDC
		• From Aug to Dec 2021	• Phase 1: Focusing on research and testing of CBDCs' basic role	• Domestic PVP
		• From Jan to June 2022	• Phase 2: Focusing on more advanced features such as privacy protection, cross-border payments, offline payments, and integration with digital asset systems	• Domestic PVP, cross-border PVP, and privacy
BOL	Research		• Conducting comprehensive studies on CBDCs	
BOT	POC (Project Inthanon)			• Wholesale CBDC
		• 2018	• Phase 1: Wholesale payment system on DLT (Corda)	• Domestic PVP
		• 2019	• Phase 2: Securities settlement on DLT (Corda)	• Domestic DVP

continued on next page

Table 9   *continued*

Central Bank	App. Level (Project)	Period	Scope of Work	Focus
BOT	POC (BOT-SCG-DV Project)	• 2020	• Connecting CBDC with business applications: CBDC life cycle management such as issuance, destruction, distribution, and payment transfer; integration with a blockchain solution for the payments in the supply chain called Procurement-to-Pay (B2P); invoice tokenization; and programmable money, a CBDC assigned with pre-defined payment conditions among parties (Hyperledger Besu)	• Retail CBDC • Payments for domestic corporates
BOT	Pilot	• Q4 2022	• Pilot testing of a retail CBDC: evaluating CBDC in conducting cash-like activities within a limited scale such as accepting, converting, or paying for goods and services • Exploring technologies other than DLT	• Retail CBDC
BSP	Research	• Started in 2020	• Formed a technical working group to conduct comprehensive CBDC study in 2020 and continuing studies on CBDC use cases	
HKMA	POC (Project LionRock)	 • 2017 • 2017	 • Phase a: Wholesale payment system on DLT (Corda) • Phase b: Securities settlement on DLT (Corda)	• Wholesale CBDC • Domestic PVP • Domestic DVP
BOT and HKMA	POC (Project Inthanon-LionRock)	 • 2019 • 2020	• Joint project of the BOT and the HKMA • Phase 1: Cross-border, cross-currency wholesale payment on DLT (Corda) • Phase 2: Cross-border, cross-currency wholesale payment on DLT (Hyperledger Besu)	• Wholesale CBDC • Cross-border, cross-currency (bilateral) PVP • Cross-border, cross-currency (multilateral) PVP
MAS	POC (Project Ubin)	 • 2017 • 2017 • 2018 • 2019	 • Phase 1: Wholesale payment system on DLT (Ethereum) • Phase 2: Wholesale payment system with liquidity saving mechanism on DLT; and three different DLT models (Corda, Hyperledger, and Quorum) developed • Phase 3: DVP across different DLTs (Quorum vs. Anquan BC [Anquan], Ethereum vs. Hyperledger [Deloitte], and Hyperledger vs. Chain Inc [Nasdaq]) • Phase 4 [Joint work with the Bank of Canada's Project Jasper]: Cross-border, cross-currency wholesale payment on DLT (Corda in Canada vs. Quorum in Singapore)	• Wholesale CBDC • Domestic PVP • Domestic PVP • Domestic DVP; and technologies comparison and verification • Cross-border, cross-currency (bilateral) PVP

continued on next page

Table 9   *continued*

Central Bank	App. Level (Project)	Period	Scope of Work	Focus
		• 2020	• Phase 5: Developing a prototype blockchain-based domestic multi-currency payment network for multiple industries utilizing blockchain use cases across industries	• Payments for domestic corporates
PBOC	Pilot	• 2019	• Running pilot e-CNY programs in some representative regions • Design features: (1) two-tier system; (2) combining centralized and distributed technological architecture; (3) both as an account-based and a value-based system; (4) non-interest accrual; (5) anonymity for small value and traceable for high value	• Retail CBDC
BOT, HKMA, And DCI of PBOC (jointly with CBUAE and BIS IH)	POC (Multiple CBDC Bridge Project [mBridge])	• Started in 2021	• Developing a POC prototype to facilitate real-time cross-border foreign exchange payments on DLT • Built on the work under Project Inthanon-LionRock	• Wholesale CBDC • Cross-border, cross-currency (multilateral) PVP
MAS and BNM (jointly with RBA, SARB, BIS IH)	POC (Project Dunbar)	• Started in 2021	• Developing technical prototypes for shared platforms on Corda and Quorum to enable international settlements using multiple CBDCs • Exploring different governance and operating designs to enable sharing of CBDC platforms	• Wholesale CBDC • Cross-border, cross-currency (multilateral) PVP

ASEAN+3 = Association of Southeast Asian Nations plus the People's Republic of China, Japan, and the Republic of Korea; BI = Bank Indonesia; BIS IH = Bank for International Settlements Innovation Hub; BNM = Bank Negara Malaysia; BOJ = Bank of Japan; BOK = Bank of Korea; BOL = Bank of Lao PDR; BOT = Bank of Thailand; BSP = Bangko Sentral ng Pilipinas; CBDC = central bank digital currency; CBUAE = the Central Bank of the United Arab Emirates; DCI of PBOC = the Digital Currency Institute of the People's Bank of China; DLT = distributed ledger technology; DV = Digital Ventures; DVP = delivery-versus-payment; ECB = European Central Bank; HKMA = Hong Kong Monetary Authority; MAS = Monetary Authority of Singapore; PBOC = People's Bank of China; POC = proof of concept; PVP = payment-versus-payment; Q4 = fourth quarter; RBA = Reserve Bank of Australia; SARB = South African Reserve Bank; SCG = Siam Cement Group.

Sources: ABMI 2021 CSIF member survey; websites and white papers of central banks; www.cbdctracker.org; and press releases.

Box 3: Wholesale Central Bank Digital Currency Projects Outside the ASEAN+3 Region

According to a Bank of International Settlements report, 23 central banks worldwide were working on wholesale central bank digital currency (CBDC) as of 1 October 2021.[a] Table B3 illustrates several wholesale CBDC initiatives of central banks located outside the Association of Southeast Asian Nations plus the People's Republic of China, Japan, and the Republic of Korea (ASEAN+3) region. Their approaches to CBDC are not significantly different from those in the region, and regional efforts to create CBDC have never lagged behind those in other regions.

Table B3: Examples of Wholesale Central Bank Digital Currency Projects Outside ASEAN+3

Jurisdiction	App. Level (Project)	Period	Scope of Work	Focus
Canada	POC (Project Jasper)	• 2017 • 2017 • 2018 • 2019	• Phase 1: Wholesale payment on DLT (Ethereum) • Phase 2: Wholesale payment on DLT (Corda) • Phase 3: Listed equities settlement on DLT (Corda) • Phase 4: (Jasper–Ubin) Cross-border, cross-currency wholesale payment on DLT (Corda in Canada vs. Quorum in Singapore)	• Domestic PVP • Domestic PVP • Domestic DVP • Cross-border, cross-currency (bilateral) PVP
Saudi Arabia and the UAE	POC (Project Aber)	• 2019	• A DLT-based single dual-issued digital currency payment system for domestic and cross-border settlement between the two countries: cross-border settlement between the two central banks; domestic settlement between three commercial banks in each country; and cross-border transactions between the commercial banks using the digital currency (Hyperledger)	• Both domestic and cross-border PVP with single currency
South Africa	(Project Khokha) • POC • Pilot	• 2018 • 2021–	• Phase 1: Wholesale payment on DLT (Quorum) • Phase 2: Issuance and settlement of debentures on DLT using securities tokenization, a wholesale CBDC, and a wholesale digital settlement token (a privately issued Stablecoin used for interbank settlement) to seek the policy and regulatory implications of tokenization in financial markets	• Domestic PVP • Domestic DVP
Switzerland (Jointly with BIS IH)	POC (Project Helvetia)	• 2020 • 2020	• Phase 1: Issuing a wholesale CBDC onto a distributed digital asset platform of SIX Digital Exchange for digital asset settlements (Corda) • Phase 2: Linking the digital asset platform to the existing wholesale payment system for the settlement of digital assets	• Domestic DVP • Demonstrating the feasibility of both settlement alternatives for digital assets
Switzerland/France (Jointly with BIS IH)	Experimental research (Project Jura)	• 2021–	• Cross-border settlement with two wholesale CBDCs (a euro wCBDC and a Swiss franc wCBDC) and a French digital financial asset on DLT (Corda) • Built on Project Helvetia	• Cross-border, cross-currency (bilateral) PVP and DVP

ASEAN+3 = Association of Southeast Asian Nations plus the People's Republic of China, Japan, and the Republic of Korea; BIS IH = Bank for International Settlements Innovation Hub; DLT = distributed ledger technology; DVP = delivery-versus-payment; POC = proof of concept; PVP = payment-versus-payment; UAE = United Arab Emirates.

[a] Bank of International Settlements (BIS). 2021. *BIS Working Paper.* No. 880. https://www.bis.org/publ/work880.htm.
Sources: Websites and papers of central banks; www.cbdctracker.org; and press releases.

C. Artificial Intelligence

The survey discovered that two central banks and one CSD in the region were experimenting with the use of AI technologies in their systems as of July 2021: one POC and one production case (Figure 32).

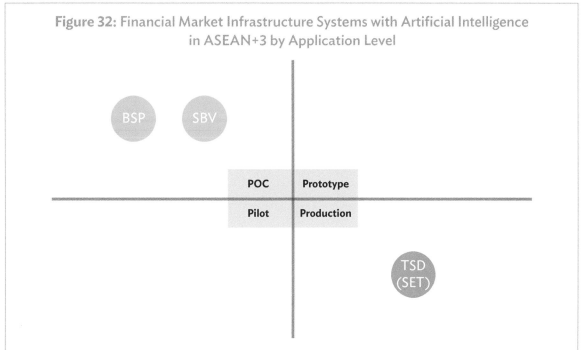

Figure 32: Financial Market Infrastructure Systems with Artificial Intelligence in ASEAN+3 by Application Level

ASEAN+3 = Association of Southeast Asian Nations plus the People's Republic of China, Japan, and the Republic of Korea; BSP = Bangko Sentral ng Pilipinas; POC = proof of concept; SBV = State Bank of Vietnam; SET = Stock Exchange of Thailand; TSD = Thailand Securities Depository.

Legend: ● central bank; and ● central securities depository.

Source: 2021 ABMI CSIF member survey.

As previously indicated, there is little doubt that full-grown AI, when combined with techniques such as graphic processing units, sequential learning, and transfer learning—on top of conceptual frameworks including deep learning and neural networks—will influence practically every industry in the economy in the foreseeable future. AI can prop up the resilience and efficiency of critical FMI in a variety of ways: it can streamline and automate post-trade processes, thereby increasing cost efficiency; provide advanced compliance and risk management capabilities; and facilitate the development of value-added data analytics solutions.

However, because AI is still in its early phase, with new sub-technologies and concepts emerging constantly, there are certain limitations to the current level of AI technologies that can't be ignored. The most significant hurdle of AI is its inability to learn to think creatively. AI is smart enough to learn over time using pre-fed data and prior experiences, but it can only respond in a predetermined manner to a conceived situation, limiting its ability to be creative. In other words, any flaws in the data and weaknesses in the programmed algorithms in an AI system will manifest themselves in the outcomes.

Besides, developing and maintaining an AI system capable of simulating human intelligence needs a lot of time and resources and can be highly expensive. These are why FMIs such as central banks and CSDs in the region, and probably most central banks and CSDs around the world, are cautious about incorporating AI technology into their systems.

As shown in Table 10, the State Bank of Vietnam (SBV), the country's central bank, is experimenting with AI in combination with big data analytics on its high-value payment system and websites to improve cybersecurity and the development and operation of IT systems. Also, in Thailand, TSD deployed an advisory chatbot in early 2021 as part of its registrar service (Box 4). Meanwhile, in the Philippines, the BSP has been exploring to advance engagements with potential providers of blockchain analyzer solutions that could facilitate, among others, surveillance of supervised financial institutions utilizing cryptocurrencies and blockchain technology in their businesses (i.e., virtual asset service providers).

Table 10: Financial Market Infrastructure Systems with Artificial Intelligence in ASEAN+3

	Institution	System	App. Level	Period	Description
CB	BSP	Blockchain Analyzer for Virtual Asset Service Providers	POC	• 2022–	• AI-enabled solutions, which apply data analytics to uncover insights on various transactional behaviors such as activities related to money laundering, terrorist financing, fraud, and other financial crimes using blockchain data from virtual asset service providers and other cryptocurrency domains
	SBV	Data analytics platform for IBPS and websites	POC	• Jul–Oct 2020 • Testing for production: Ongoing since Jul 2021	• Cloud based, AI-powered data analytics platform for SBV IPBS's cybersecurity and DevOps, as well as SBV's websites • POC of AI and big data analytics
CSD	TSD (SET)	Registrar Advisory Bot	Production	• 2020– launched in Feb 2021	• Chatbot registrar services for listed companies appointed TSD as registrar

AI = artificial intelligence; ASEAN+3 = Association of Southeast Asian Nations plus the People's Republic of China, Japan, and the Republic of Korea; BSP = Bangko Sentral ng Pilipinas; CB = central bank; CSD = central securities depository; IBPS = Inter-Bank Electronic Payment System; POC = proof of concept; SBV = State Bank of Vietnam; SET = Stock Exchange of Thailand; TSD = Thailand Securities Depository.
Source: ABMI 2021 CSIF member survey.

Box 4: Thailand Securities Depository's Registrar Advisory Bot

Thailand Securities Depository's (TSD) Registrar Advisory Bot is a keyword recognition-based chatbot, providing information related to various corporate processing actions such as cut-off time of activities and document preparation, with listed equity issuers that appointed TSD as registrar through Q&A (Figure B4).

Figure B4: Thailand Securities Depository's Registrar Advisory Bot

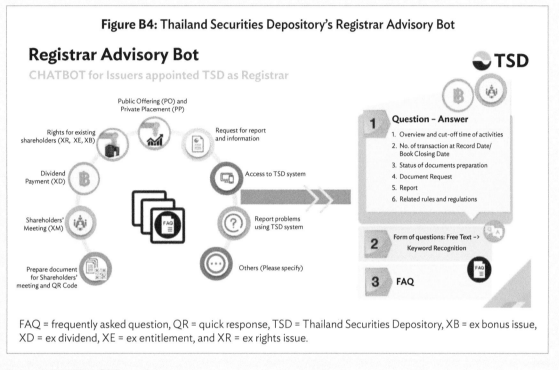

FAQ = frequently asked question, QR = quick response, TSD = Thailand Securities Depository, XB = ex bonus issue, XD = ex dividend, XE = ex entitlement, and XR = ex rights issue.

Source: ABMI 2021 CSIF member survey.

D. Big Data Analytics

As for the big data analytics, it is found that two central banks and three CSDs have explored or implemented the technology: SBV and BNM each have a POC and a production case; PT Kustodian Sentral Efek Indonesia (KSEI)—the Indonesian CSD—has two production cases; Shanghai Clearing House (SHCH), one of the PRC's CSDs that provides custody and settlement for corporate bonds, has a pilot case; and the Vietnam Securities Depository (VSD) has a production case (Figure 33).

In terms of central banks, Malaysia's BNM has recently enhanced the data analytics capability of RENTAS (BNM's RTGS) to analyze various potential scenarios such as liquidity shock, technology outage, and market impact. In the near future, BNM intends to shift toward data lake infrastructure to harness the full potential of cloud computing upon finalizing the cloud framework. In Viet Nam, SBV is experimenting with AI-based big data analytics on its interbank payment system, as mentioned previously in the AI section. In Indonesia, KSEI launched a surveillance system in 2019 and has gradually implemented big data to support analysis and decision-making since 2021. In the PRC, SHCH is also

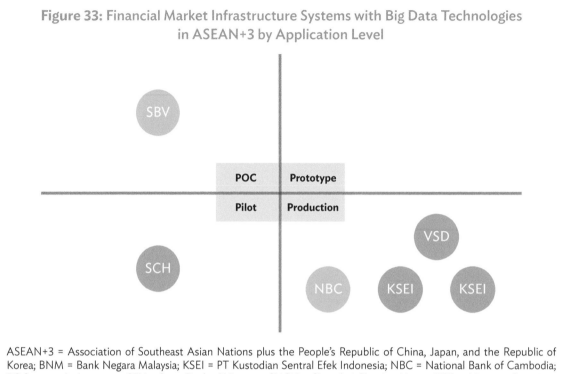

Figure 33: Financial Market Infrastructure Systems with Big Data Technologies in ASEAN+3 by Application Level

ASEAN+3 = Association of Southeast Asian Nations plus the People's Republic of China, Japan, and the Republic of Korea; BNM = Bank Negara Malaysia; KSEI = PT Kustodian Sentral Efek Indonesia; NBC = National Bank of Cambodia; POC = proof of concept; SBV = State Bank of Vietnam; SHCH = Shanghai Clearing House; VSD = Vietnam Securities Depository.

Legend: ● central bank; and ● central securities depository.

Source: 2021 ABMI CSIF member survey.

piloting a data analysis platform to leverage AI to address a variety of business concerns. Finally, VSD built a security information and event management (SIEM) system in Viet Nam in 2018 that harnesses big data technology to automate data analysis processes, thereby increasing its response to cyber threats (Table 11).

Although certain era-defining technologies such as big data analytics, AI, and cloud computing are distinct technologies that developed and evolved independently, they are far from being employed in isolation in the real world. The convergence of these technologies creates new opportunities and accelerates the digital transformation of enterprises, significantly increasing processing capacity. AI empowers machines to do specific tasks based on data-driven user insights, and cloud computing promotes the use of big data analytics by giving anytime, anywhere access to data via cloud servers. As a result, the distinctions between these technologies are getting increasingly blurred. Further, big data and AI technologies are frequently integrated into various cybersecurity technology solutions. This phenomenon is also evident among CSIF members: SBV's POC for a cloud-based and AI-powered data analytics platform, SHCH's pilot for a data analytics platform that will incorporate AI technology, and VSD's cybersecurity solution that combines big data technologies (Table 11).

Table 11: Financial Market Infrastructure Systems with Big Data Technologies in ASEAN+3

	Institution	System	App. Level	Period	Description
CB	BNM	Data analytics platform	Production	• 2021	• Use of data analytics on RENTAS (national RTGS) data to expand supervisory surveillance and obtain better data permutation to facilitate policy-making • Open-source based tools such as Grafana and Kibana for data visualization on technology resilience and languages such as R or Python
	SBV	Data analytics platform for IBPS and websites	POC	• Jul–Oct 2020 • Started testing for production in Jul 2021	• Cloud based, AI-powered data analytics platform for SBV IBPS's cybersecurity and DevOps, as well as SBV's websites • POC of AI and big data analytics
CSD	KSEI	Surveillance system	Production	• 2019	• Leveraging big data analytics to support internal surveillance process
		Big data-based management support system	Production	• 2021	• Started to utilize big data to support management decision-making via swift data provision and analysis
	SHCH	Data Statistics and Analysis Platform	Pilot		• Piloting to realize the unified data management and analysis • Planning to apply AI technology to tackle various business issues
	VSD	SIEM for IT operation management	Production	• Launched in Feb 2018	• To collect and analyze security logs automatically • Application case of both big data analytics to a cybersecurity technology solution

AI = artificial intelligence; ASEAN+3 = Association of Southeast Asian Nations plus the People's Republic of China, Japan, and the Republic of Korea; BNM = Bank Negara Malaysia; CB = central bank; CSD = central securities depository; IBPS = Inter-Bank Electronic Payment System; IT = information technology; KSEI = PT Kustodian Sentral Efek Indonesia; POC = proof of concept; RTGS = real-time gross settlement; SBV = State Bank of Vietnam; SHCH = Shanghai Clearing House; SIEM = security information and event management; VSD = Vietnam Securities Depository.

Source: ABMI 2021 CSIF member survey.

E. Cloud Computing

In cloud computing, only BSP and SBV have application cases. BSP has one under POC, while SBV has one for production and one for prototyping (Figure 34). These findings appear to mirror the challenges inherent in cloud adoption such as security and compliance concerns, efficient cloud spending, and cloud adoption and data transfer (see page 37, Benefits and Challenges).

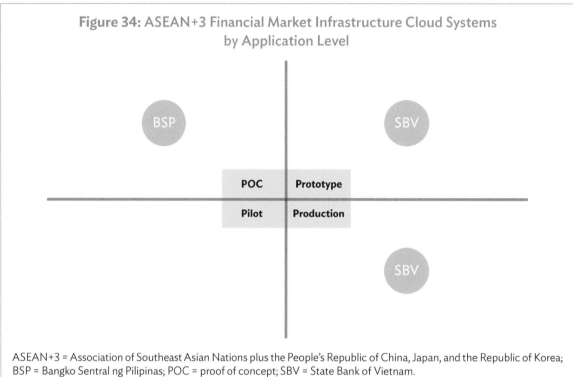

Figure 34: ASEAN+3 Financial Market Infrastructure Cloud Systems by Application Level

ASEAN+3 = Association of Southeast Asian Nations plus the People's Republic of China, Japan, and the Republic of Korea; BSP = Bangko Sentral ng Pilipinas; POC = proof of concept; SBV = State Bank of Vietnam.
Legend: ● central bank; and ● central securities depository.
Source: 2021 ABMI CSIF member survey.

SBV has adopted public cloud for its e-government applications and is evaluating a prototype public cloud platform for its public services provided by the Ministry of Information and Communication. Meanwhile, BSP is exploring a unified regulatory and supervisory technology end-to-end solution to streamline and automate regulatory supervision, reporting, and compliance assessment of cybersecurity risk management of BSP-supervised financial institutions. It is envisioned as a cloud-hosted platform where all BSP-supervised financial institutions can directly access and transmit cybersecurity-related reports and information real-time (Table 12).

Table 12: Financial Market Infrastructure Systems with Cloud Systems in ASEAN+3

	Institution	System	App. Level	Period	Description
CB	BSP	Advanced Supervisory Technology Engine for Risk-Based Compliance (ASTERisC)	POC	• Started in 2022	• The system shall support BSP's end-to-end process on cybersecurity supervision and oversight from cyber-profiling, cyber incident reporting, cybersecurity control self-assessments as well as correlating with results of on-site supervision and inspection
	SBV	Electronic Government	Production		• Introduced public cloud services for e-Government applications
		Public Cloud	Prototype	• Scheduled to be completed by 2024	• To introduce cloud services for SBV's public services • Initially considered using private cloud but switched to public cloud • Currently testing and evaluating a public cloud provided by MIC for rollout under the SBV Web portal project 2024

ASEAN+3 = Association of Southeast Asian Nations plus the People's Republic of China, Japan, and the Republic of Korea; BSP = Bangko Sentral ng Pilipinas; CB = central bank; MIC = Ministry of Information and Communication; POC = proof of concept; SBV = State Bank of Vietnam.
Source: ABMI 2021 CSIF member survey.

F. Cybersecurity

For cybersecurity, eight CSIF member institutions, four central banks, and four CSDs answered they are protecting their systems either with new cybersecurity technologies implemented or following international cybersecurity standards as an FMI (Figure 35).

FMIs must operate safely and efficiently to maintain and promote financial stability and economic prosperity. Unless adequately managed, FMIs can be a cause of financial shocks. Cyber resilience, which adds to an FMI's operational resilience, can be a critical element in the financial system's and larger economy's overall resilience. In this context, cybersecurity is one of the top priorities of all central banks and CSDs in the region. Understandably, security concerns would be the primary reason that majority of the CSIF member institutions did not provide the cybersecurity features of their systems. Table 13 summarizes the responses of the CSIF members.

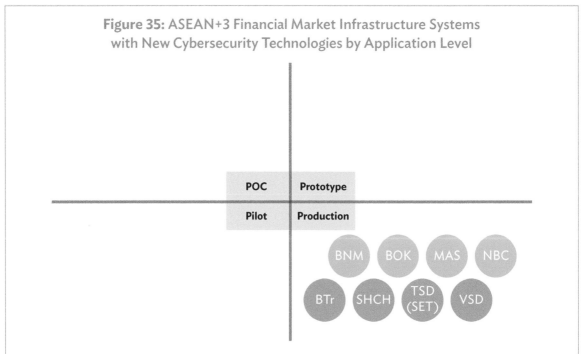

Figure 35: ASEAN+3 Financial Market Infrastructure Systems with New Cybersecurity Technologies by Application Level

ASEAN+3 = Association of Southeast Asian Nations plus the People's Republic of China, Japan, and the Republic of Korea; BOK = Bank of Korea; BTr = Bureau of Treasury; MAS = Monetary Authority of Singapore; NBC = National Bank of Cambodia; POC = proof of concept; SET = Stock Exchange of Thailand; SHCH = Shanghai Clearing House; TSD = Thailand Securities Depository; VSD = Vietnam Securities Depository.

Legend: ● central bank; and ● central securities depository.

Source: 2021 ABMI CSIF member survey.

Table 13: Financial Market Infrastructure Systems with New Cybersecurity Technologies in ASEAN+3

	Institution	System	App. Level	Period	Description
CB	BNM	CSD and RTGS systems	Production	• SIEM: Launched in 2018 • PAM: Launched in 2018 • APT: Launched in 2018 • SOC: Extended to 24/7 in 2020 • Other initiatives have been deployed since 2018 continuously	• Adopted new technologies such as anti-APT, privileged access management and set up of 24/7 security operations center • Advancements in the cybersecurity domain are in line with recommendations from primary cybersecurity frameworks • Implementation details of techs cannot be shared due to sensitivity.

continued on next page

Table 13   *continued*

	Institution	System	App. Level	Period	Description
	BOK	BOK-Wire+ (RTGS)	Production	• SIEM developed: Sep–Dec 2018 • SIEM launched: Jan 2019 • SIEM upgraded: Jul–Sep 2020	• Implemented SIEM to analyze the big data collected from firewall, IPS, antivirus S/W logs to tackle cyberattack and abnormal activities on a real-time basis • Additionally adopted anti-APT solution to protect IT systems from the cyberattacks effectively
	MAS	MEPS+ (RTGS)	Production		• Adopted technology tools, following the guideline of Principles of Financial Market Infrastructures • Implementation details of techs cannot be shared due to sensitivity
	NBC	Bakong payment system ("Project Bakong")	Production	• Project Bakong launched in Oct 2020	• Follows the National Institute of Standards and Technology cybersecurity framework
CSD	BTr	National Registry of Scripless Securities (NRoSS)	Production	• NRoSS launched in Aug 2018	• Cybersecurity solutions applied as an important financial market infrastructure
	SHCH	All market systems	Production		• Cybersecurity solutions applied as an important financial market infrastructure
	TSD (SET)	CSD and Registrar systems	Production	• ISO 20000 and ISO 27001 certified: 2019 • ISO 27701 certified: 2020	• Complies international standards for IT security such as ISO 20000 (IT Service Management), ISO 27001 (Information Security Management) and ISO 27701 (Privacy Information Management)
	VSD	IT operation management	Production	• SIEM launched in Feb 2018	• Implemented SIEM to collect and analyze security logs automatically • Application case of both big data analytics to a cybersecurity technology solution

APT = advanced persistent threat; ASEAN+3 = Association of Southeast Asian Nations plus the People's Republic of China, Japan, and the Republic of Korea; BNM = Bank Negara Malaysia; BOK = Bank of Korea; BTr = Bureau of Treasury; CB = central bank; CSD = central securities depository; IPS = intrusion prevention system; ISO = International Organization for Standardization; IT = information technology; MAS = Monetary Authority of Singapore; MEPS = MAS Electronic Payment System; NBC = National Bank of Cambodia; PAM = Privileged Access Management; RTGS = real-time gross settlement; SET = Stock Exchange of Thailand; SHCH = Shanghai Clearing House; SIEM = security information and event management; SOC = security operation center; TSD = Thailand Securities Depository; VSD = Vietnam Securities Depository.

Source: ABMI 2021 CSIF member survey.

G. (Open) Application Programming Interfaces

(Open) API has been identified as the technology most widely applied in CSIF member institutions' systems. With seven central banks and three CSDs, the region has seen 10 application cases: two POCs, one prototype, and seven production cases. Seven of the 10 instances involve central banks, and the remaining three include CSDs (Figure 36).

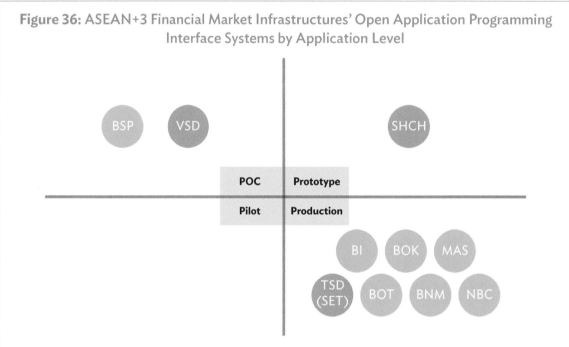

Figure 36: ASEAN+3 Financial Market Infrastructures' Open Application Programming Interface Systems by Application Level

ASEAN+3 = Association of Southeast Asian Nations plus the People's Republic of China, Japan, and the Republic of Korea; BI = Bank Indonesia; BNM = Bank Negara Malaysia; BOK = Bank of Korea; BOT = Bank of Thailand; BSP = Bangko Sentral ng Pilipinas; MAS = Monetary Authority of Singapore; NBC = National Bank of Cambodia; POC = proof of concept; SET = Stock Exchange of Thailand; SHCH = Shanghai Clearing House; TSD = Thailand Securities Depository; VSD = Vietnam Securities Depository.

Legend: ● central bank; and ● central securities depository.

Source: 2021 ABMI CSIF member survey.

Limited to CSIF members, it appears that the region's central banks are embracing APIs more actively for both their systems and markets. This is likely because open banking, one of the growing "open X" ecosystems, is rapidly gaining traction in the banking sector globally, and policymakers in the region have begun incorporating open banking into their financial markets. Certain members, including BOK and TSD, embraced APIs as early as 2013 and 2014. Table 14 highlights the adoption of APIs by CSIF members.

APIs provide potent resources for rapid system development and facilitate the integration and interoperability of various software applications with fewer resources. APIs have the potential to catalyze disruptive innovation and uncover new revenue streams for businesses. On the other hand, security might be an issue, as APIs offer another potential attack layer to programs and websites.

Also, developing and implementing API capabilities can be costly in terms of development time and continuing maintenance requirements. When organizations use different APIs, they exacerbate market inefficiencies and impede interoperability. This is why API standardization is crucial to accelerating market growth. The region's central banks—such as BI, BNM, and the BSP—recognize the benefits of open API standardization for their industry as a whole and are taking steps to promote wider adoption of open APIs.

Table 14: Financial Market Infrastructure Systems with (Open) Application Programming Interface in ASEAN+3

	Institution	System	App. Level	Period	Description
CB	BI	SNAP-based Open API payment systems [Run by PSPs and PSOs]	Production	• Consultative paper on SNAP published in Q1 2020 • SNAP development site created in Jun 2021 • SNAP enacted in Aug 2021 • SNAP-based open API payment systems: To be fully implemented by Q2 2022	• To facilitate collaboration between the banking and FinTech industries through open banking, BI enforced in August 2021 the National Open API Payment Standards (SNAP), which will be applied to payment service providers (PSPs) and payment system operators (PSOs). • SNAP includes technical and security standards, data standards, and governance standards of an open API payment system. • To promote the industry-wide SNAP implementation, BI has created a SNAP developer site, providing online sandbox applications to facilitate development trials and support the piloting phase of SNAP-based open API payment systems.
	BNM	Information provision via open API	Production	• Launched in 2019	• BNM established the Open API Implementation Group in March 2018 to identify and develop standardized APIs for high-impact use cases, particularly on product information in relation to SME financing, credit card, and motor insurance (takaful). • In January 2019, BNM issued a policy document, Publishing Open Data using Open API. The policy document sets out BNM's recommendations to the industry in developing and publishing open APIs on publicly available data. The recommendations include design considerations for open APIs as well as security measures to protect against cybersecurity threats, which are proportionate to the sensitivity of data being shared through open APIs.

continued on next page

Table 14 *continued*

Institution	System	App. Level	Period	Description
				• Open APIs are used to serve the public by allowing faster, more efficient, and secure access to data including information such as foreign currency exchange and money services reports. • BNM will explore future application of open API for RENTAS (national RTGS), in accordance with business requirements and needs.
BOK	Economic Statistic System	Production	• Developed since Apr 2013 • Launched in Dec 2013	• A system to disclose economic statistics data that the BOK generated and collected. • Implemented in 2013 to fulfill the Open Government Data Policy and facilitate effective use of the statistics for users utilizing open API.
BOT	BAHTNET API	Production	• Launched in Nov 2020	• Implemented to track the status of BAHTNET (BOT's RTGS system) transactions, enabling BAHTNET participants to notify their customers of fund deposit in a timely manner. • BOT will extend the use of open APIs to enable straight-through-processing in the BAHTNET system.
BSP	Real-time analytics dashboard and report engine [Run by BSP] Open finance platforms [Run by BSFIs]	POC	• Scheduled to be completed by Q4 2022	• To promote open finance among BSP-supervised financial institutions (BSFIs) and third-party providers, the BSP issued in June 2021 the Open Finance Framework, which covers technology, products, services, information, and policies for open finance. • Uses open APIs for banks (BSFIs) to exchange customer and product information and transactions, and for BSP to have real-time analytics and reporting
MAS	API payment gateway [Run by DFWG]	Production	• Launched in Nov 2020	• Developed by the Direct FAST Working Group (DFWG) as an alternative connectivity model for the participating financial institutions to FAST (Singapore's real-time retail payment system) and PayNow (an addressing service allowing participants of FAST to use their identifiers such as mobile numbers to make FAST transfers).

continued on next page

Table 14 *continued*

	Institution	System	App. Level	Period	Description
	NBC	Bakong payment system ("Project Bakong")	Production	• Project Bakong launched in Oct 2020	• Uses open APIs to connect all payment service institutions (PSIs) with Bakong • Introduced public mobile application to eliminate the need for banks and PSIs to develop their own while allowing those with an existing mobile application to integrate via open API easily
CSD	SHCH	Open Platform for Data Interface	Prototype		
	TSD (SET)	CSD systems	Production	• Developed since 2012 • Launched in 2014	• Uses a FIX API to exchange data with TSD participants
	VSD	Corporate action information auto collection system	POC	• Under development since Feb 2021	• VSD participants automatically collects and processes corporate action information on the VSD website • Uses Restful Web API

API = application programming interface; ASEAN+3 = Association of Southeast Asian Nations plus the People's Republic of China, Japan, and the Republic of Korea; BI = Bank Indonesia; BNM = Bank Negara Malaysia; BOK = Bank of Korea; BOT = Bank of Thailand; BSP = Bangko Sentral ng Pilipinas; CB = central bank; CSD = central securities depository; FinTech = financial technology; FIX = Financial Information eXchange; MAS = Monetary Authority of Singapore; NBC = National Bank of Cambodia; POC = proof of concept; Q1 = first quarter; Q4 = fourth quarter; RTGS = real-time gross settlement; SET = Stock Exchange of Thailand; SHCH = Shanghai Clearing House; SME = small and medium-sized enterprise; TSD = Thailand Securities Depository; VSD = Vietnam Securities Depository.

Note: Descriptions of the concepts of "open banking" and "open finance" can be found on page 50, Application Programming Interface-Powered Digital Transformation.

Sources: ABMI 2021 CSIF member survey; press releases, policy documents, white papers, and websites of each institution.

Box 5 illustrates TSD's implementation of FIX API as part of its CSD system.

Box 5: Thailand Securities Depository's Implementation of a Financial Information eXchange Application Programming Interface

Thailand Securities Depository (TSD) implemented a financial information eXchange (FIX) application programming interface (API) engine since FIX protocol is the most widely used among capital market participants for real-time communication, and the FIX API is primarily used by FIX protocol users.

TSD's messaging through the FIX API covers (i) account and shareholder management, (ii) account transfer, (iii) securities deposit and withdrawal, (iv) foreign exchange information, (v) over-the-counter bond settlement, and (vi) securities profile.

Figure B5: Thailand Securities Depository's FIX API

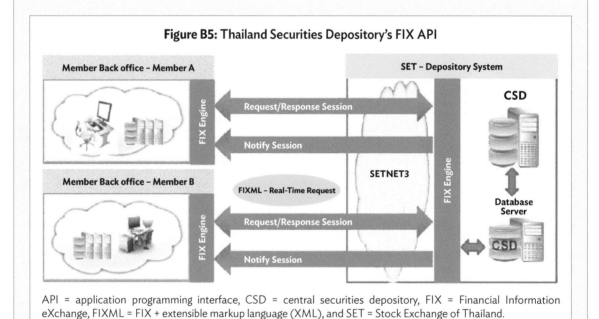

API = application programming interface, CSD = central securities depository, FIX = Financial Information eXchange, FIXML = FIX + extensible markup language (XML), and SET = Stock Exchange of Thailand.

Source: ABMI 2021 CSIF member survey.

IV Application of New Technologies to a Regional Settlement Intermediary Model: CSD–RTGS Linkages

Based on the survey results and desktop studies conducted by the CSIF Secretariat, 16 of the 20 CSIF member institutions that responded to the survey have experimented, are experimenting, or have implemented at least one of the six new technologies applicable to FMIs: DLT, AI, big data analytics, cloud computing, new cybersecurity techniques, and (open) APIs.

When the number of application cases for each of the six new technologies is considered, (open) APIs had the most, with 10: eight each in DLT and cybersecurity, six in big data analytics, and three each in AI and cloud computing. In the case of production, eight cases for cybersecurity and seven cases for (open) API were discovered, as well as three cases each in DLT and big data analytics, and one each for AI and cloud computing.

Many application cases in cybersecurity and (open) API are observed because, to a systemically important FMI, even minor security vulnerabilities within a security system are important issues that cannot be ignored. And there is great demand for business process automation to improve operational efficiency and interconnection among independent business systems for new business opportunities— such as open banking or open finance—under the digitizing business environment. Also, the number of application cases for DLT and big data analytics is not small. DLT has the potential to fundamentally alter the existing centralized business model of FMIs, which is why many FMIs around the world are rushing to explore the technology. In the case of big data analytics, the demand for utilizing massive volumes of data accumulated within each FMI is increasing. However, application cases of AI and cloud computing in the region remain few, most likely due to concerns about AI's technological immaturity and cloud computing's security.

CSD–RTGS Linkages, an RSI model, was designed through CSIF discussions to promote safe and efficient intraregional cross-border financial transactions by directly linking settlement systems of central banks and CSDs in the region. Thus, all six new technologies that are used by the region's central banks and CSD systems can also be deployed to this linkage model, albeit at different moments in time. In the short term, DLT combined with (open) APIs and cloud computing can be a viable target for application. DLT can serve as the foundation for the development of a multipurpose FMI platform that registered and regulated entities may utilize to transact and manage assets in a more efficient, more transparent, manner. Adopting a technically feasible, scalable, and decentralized governance structure enabled by DLT could alleviate participating member markets from the geopolitical hegemony dilemma inherent in centralized regional market infrastructure. Cloud computing, (open) APIs, and cybersecurity technologies would all be required to ensure the linked system's ubiquity, interoperability, and security. From a longer-term perspective, the remaining two technologies, AI and big data analytics, can be implemented as needed.

The CSIF Secretariat is currently engaged in a project of exploring the redesign of CSD–RTGS linkages using DLT to benefit CSIF member institutions. The to-be created DLT-based linkage model is envisaged to serve as a baseline for CSIF members' future development of DLT-based market infrastructure. The project outcome will be released in a separate report once completed.

New Technology Stock-Taking Survey Questionnaire of CSIF Members

---

QUESTIONNAIRE

NEW TECHNOLOGIES-APPLIED MARKET SYSTEMS

1.1. Has your organization applied, or been applying, any of the technologies below to your market infrastructure system(s)? (Multiple choices available. If there is (are), go to Q1. (2), if none, go to Q3)

( ) DLT(blockchain) with/without a coin/token ( ) Cloud computing ( ) Cybersecurity
( ) Artificial intelligence (AI) ( ) Big data analytics ( ) Open API

1.2. Are there other innovative technologies that you would like to point out than the ones mentioned in Q1 (1), applied, being applied, or applicable to your market infrastructure system(s)? if yes, please specify.

( ) Yes ( ) No

1.3. What is a target market system for each new technology applied or being applied and each technology's level of application?

Tech (being) applied	Market system	Application level (Mark X where applicable)			
_____	_____	( ) POC	( ) Prototype	( ) Pilot	( ) Production
_____	_____	( ) POC	( ) Prototype	( ) Pilot	( ) Production
_____	_____	( ) POC	( ) Prototype	( ) Pilot	( ) Production

To answer Q2, if possible, CSIF member institutions are encouraged to just provide any type of description materials including presentations in PowerPoint or operation manuals containing information asked, for each new technology-applied market system.

2.1. Please provide the overview(s) of the market system(s) to which each new technology applies or is being applied (market function of the system(s), technical and operational structure, function and coverage of each new technology (being) applied, benefits and limits of the new system(s), possibly compared with legacy system(s), and future expansion plans or improvement requirements, etc.)

_____

_____

_____

2.2. Please provide the overview(s) of system development(s) (system launching date, period and cost of the development, obstacles faced during the development including regulatory issues, and information on outsourced vendor(s) and their package solution(s), etc.)

_____

_____

_____

2.3. Has your organization assessed or considered applying any of those technologies mentioned in Q1 to your market system(s) before, or does your organization have a plan to apply, or consider applying, in the near future? If yes, please provide details including any elements of consideration for system development.

( ) Yes   ( ) No

_____

_____

_____

OTHER QUESTIONS

3.1. [To central banks only] Has your organization issued central bank digital currency (CBDC)? If yes, please provide the details.

( ) Yes   ( ) No

_____

_____

3.2. [To central banks only] Does your organization plan to issue a CBDC in the near future? If yes, please provide the details.

( ) Yes   ( ) No

_____

_____

4.1. Does your organization have service(s) or market systems(s) to support cross-border (inbound or outbound) financial activities? If yes, please provide the details.

( ) Yes   ( ) No

_____

_____

4.2. Does your organization have a plan to provide service(s) or develop market system(s) to support cross-border (inbound or outbound) financial activities in the near future? If yes, please provide the details.

( ) Yes   ( ) No

_____

_____

Cross-Border Settlement Infrastructure Forum Members' Cross-Border Services

The survey also inquired about Cross-Border Settlement Infrastructure member organizations' cross-border financial services. There are nine members with cross-border services (seven central banks and two CSDs) and six members (four central banks and two CSDs) seeking to extend their cross-border services (Figure A2.1). However, four members (two central banks and two CSDs) responded that they do not offer cross-border services but plan to do so in the near future (Figure A2.2).

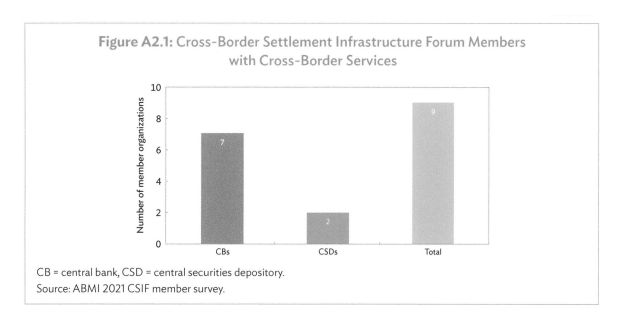

Figure A2.1: Cross-Border Settlement Infrastructure Forum Members with Cross-Border Services

CB = central bank, CSD = central securities depository.
Source: ABMI 2021 CSIF member survey.

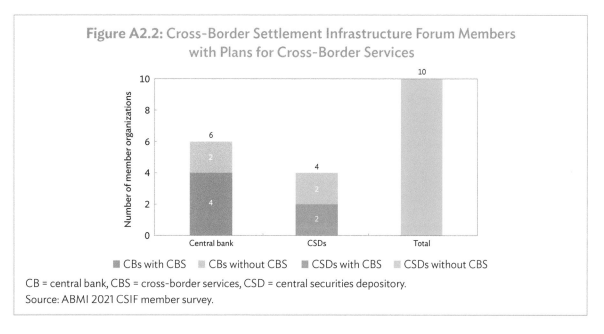

Figure A2.2: Cross-Border Settlement Infrastructure Forum Members with Plans for Cross-Border Services

CB = central bank, CBS = cross-border services, CSD = central securities depository.
Source: ABMI 2021 CSIF member survey.

Lightning Source UK Ltd.
Milton Keynes UK
UKHW050914160922
408923UK00005B/272

9 789292 695736